D1130539

TWAYNE'S WORLD AUTHORS SERIES

A Survey of the World's Literature

ROMANIA

Ion Luca Caragiale

(TWAS 276)

TWAYNE'S WORLD AUTHORS SERIES (TWAS)

The purpose of TWAS is to survey the major writers–novelists, dramatists, historians, poets, philosophers, and critics–of the nations of the world. Among the national literatures covered are those of Australia, Canada, China, Eastern Europe, France, Germany, Greece, India, Italy, Japan, Latin America, the Netherlands, New Zealand, Poland, Russia, Scandinavia, Spain, and the African nations, as well as Hebrew, Yiddish, and Latin Classical literatures. This survey is complemented by Twayne's United States Authors Series and English Authors Series.

The intent of each volume in these series is to present a critical analytical study of the works of the writer; to include biographical and historical material that may be necessary for understanding, appreciation, and critical appraisal of the writer; and to present all material in clear, concise English–but not to vitiate the scholarly content of the work by doing so.

Ion Luca Caragiale

By ERIC D. TAPPE

University of London

Twayne Publishers, Inc. :: New York

Library of Congress Catalog Card Number: 73-1669

ISBN 0-8057-2199-1

MANUFACTURED IN THE UNITED STATES OF AMERICA

Preface

If a Romanian is asked "Who has written the best Romanian play?" or "Who is the greatest Romanian comic writer?" his answer in either case is likely to be "Caragiale." On the other hand, if the question arises of presenting Caragiale's writings to the world in general, a Romanian will often express doubt whether they could have any appeal outside Romania. He will very likely maintain that they are largely untranslatable. Certainly where Caragiale's comedies and many of his sketches of contemporary Bucharest life are concerned, the flavor of the character's speech cannot be satisfactorily reproduced in another language. In a great number of sketches Caragiale has made certain aspects of life in Bucharest at the end of the nineteenth century so vivid that one comes to see Bucharest of the period in those terms, just as one sees London of fifty years earlier in terms of Dickens' fiction. It is particularly in these that the full flavor evaporates in translation; but even with this loss much is left.

There are, however, other works which seem to claim universality. If Gogol's *Revizor* is so often performed with success outside Russia, Caragiale's comedy of political intrigue in a provincial town, *O scrisoare pierdută*, should be just as appealing. And of his tales the short story "La hanul lui Mînjoală" with its irony and its subtle construction, and the delightful nouvelle *Kir Ianulea*, localizing a tale of Machiavelli's in eighteenth-century Wallachia, are worthy to take their place among the world's classics.

E. D. TAPPE

St. Leonards on Sea, Sussex

Acknowledgments

For the facts of Caragiale's life, his bibliography, and so on, this book is entirely indebted to the research of others; I do not claim to have discovered any new fact. Above all I am indebted to Professor Şerban Cioculescu, including both his well-known works and hitherto unreprinted articles which he was kind enough to lend me. He it was who carried to completion the definitive edition of Caragiale begun by Paul Zarifopol; he collaborated in the edition with commentary, of which four volumes appeared between 1959 and 1965; he wrote the standard biography. He is thus the chief figure in Caragialian studies.

For the critical side of this book I have deliberately refrained from systematic reading of Romanian literary criticism; it seemed to me that the chief interest of my study must be a response unprejudiced as far as possible by the views of native critics.

Passages translated from Caragiale bulk considerably in the text. Without them this book would be of little use to the general public since so few non-Romanians can read Romanian, while English versions are practically unobtainable. These translations are from my own hitherto unpublished versions.

E. D. T.

Contents

Chronology

1852 January 30: Ion Luca Caragiale born at Haimanale near Ploeşti in Wallachia.

1859–
1867 At school in Ploeşti.

1868 Goes to Bucharest to study declamation in the class conducted by his uncle Iorgu Caragiale.

1870 Father dies.

1871 Appointed prompter and copyist at the National Theater in Bucharest. Works also as proofreader for two newspapers.

1875 First publication, contributions to the weekly *Ghimpele* (The Thorn).

1877 May-June: brings out six numbers of a humorous weekly, *Claponul* (The Capon).

1878 May 21: his translation of the French verse tragedy *Rome vaincue* by Al. Parodi is staged at the National Theater. November 12: reads his comedy *O noapte furtunoasă* (A Stormy Night) to the literary circle *Junimea* (Youth) at Jassy on the occasion of its fifteenth anniversary.

1879 January 18: *O noapte furtunoasă* staged at the National Theater.

1880 February 1: the farce *Conu Leonida faţă cu reacţiunea* (Mr. Leonida faced with Reaction) published in Junimea's organ *Convorbiri literare* (Literary Conversations).

1881 Appointed to an inspectorship of schools in Moldavia.

1882 Transferred to an inspectorship in Wallachia.

1884 November 13: the comedy *O scrisoare pierdută* (A Lost Letter) staged at the National Theater.

1885 March 12: birth of his illegitimate son, Matei. April 8: the comedy *D-ale carnavalului* (Carnival Doings) staged at the National Theater.

1888 July 2: appointed Director General of Theaters (i.e., of the National Theater, Bucharest).

1889	January 7: marries Alexandrina Burelly. May 5: resigns directorship. His comedies printed in the volume *Teatru.*
1890	February 3: the drama *Năpasta* (False Witness) staged at the National Theater.
1891	April 14: the Romanian Academy rejects his plays for the Eliade Rădulescu prize.
1892	Quarrels with Maiorescu and ceases to contribute to *Convorbiri literare.* May 9: attacks *Junimea* in a public lecture at the Ateneu. Publishes a volume of stories, *Păcat* (Sin), and one of lighter pieces, *Note şi schiţe* (Notes and Sketches). Draws closer to the Socialist party.
1893	January-June: brings out a humorous weekly, *Moftul român* (Romanian Nonsense). July 2: birth of first legitimate child to survive infancy, a son, Luca Ion.
1894	Birth of a daughter, Ecaterina.
1895	September: joins the Radical party of G. Panu.
1896	March: with Panu joins the Conservative party of Lascar Catargi. September: unsuccessfully applies for the directorship of the National Theater at Jassy.
1898	February: "La hanul lui Mînjoală" (At Mînjoală's Inn) printed in *Gazeta săteanului* (The Villager's Gazette).
1901	February 23: banquet given by friends in honor of his twenty-five years of literary activity. April-November: second series of *Moftul român.* October 10: "La hanul lui Mînjoală" and other stories reprinted in the volume *Momente* (Moments). December 18: prosecutes C. A. Ionescu ("Caion") for accusing him of plagiarism in *Năpasta.*
1902	March 11: Caion convicted (but acquitted on retrial, June 10). March 23: Romanian Academy rejects *Momente* for the Năsturel-Herăscu prize.
1904	The Caragiale family settles in Berlin.
1905	Begins work on *Titircă, Sotirescu & C-ie*, a projected sequel to *O noapte furtunoasă* and *O scrisoare pierdută.*
1907	The brochure, *1907, Din primăvară în toamnă* (1907, From Spring to Autumn), reflections on the peasant uprisings, printed in over 10,000 copies.
1909	November: *Kir Ianulea* printed in *Viaţa românească* (Romanian Life).
1910	*Kir Ianulea* and other tales reprinted in the volume *Schiţe nouă* (New Sketches).
1912	June 9: dies at Berlin.

CHAPTER 1

Life

ROMANIA as a state did not exist when Ion Luca Caragiale was born. His birthplace was in Wallachia, one of the two Danubian Principalities–more accurately, Romanian Principalities–which at that moment were beginning for the first time to attract the attention of that educated public in Western Europe which was interested in foreign affairs. These two principalities, Wallachia and Moldavia, had been for many centuries vassal states of the Ottoman Empire. It is important to insist on their status; they were not, as was what is now Bulgaria, provinces of the empire. They had to pay tribute to the Ottoman Empire, and the election of their princes had to be ratified by its government; but the principalities retained their own laws and administration. Their development–economic, social, and political–had been retarded by this connection. Their position on the meeting point of the Ottoman, Austrian, and Russian Empires exposed them to repeated military occupations. The Turks monopolized their export of grain until 1828, after which the Russians hampered it by allowing the Sulina mouth of the Danube to silt up. Industrial growth had been stunted at birth. So had the growth of a middle class between the extremes of absentee landlords and serfs. The very language of cultivated society had ceased to be Romanian. Under the influence of Greek ruling princes appointed by the Turks in the period from 1714 to 1821, Greek had been the language of higher education. By the second quarter of the nineteenth century French was becoming the language of polite society.

During this quarter of a century between 1825 and 1850 new ideas were spreading. A progressive elite, some of whose younger members had been sent to France for the later stages of their education, were inspired with a consciousness of being "Romanians" and were working for the modernization of the principalities and for their union. There were more facilities for printing. Romanian periodicals had been started. Many translations from French and other languages had been printed, and original poetry and prose had an outlet for publication. In each principality a Romanian theater already existed by 1850, though it was furnished largely with Romanian adaptations of foreign plays.

It was into a theatrical family that Caragiale was born. His uncle Costache was the leading figure in the theaters of Wallachia and Moldavia around 1850. His father Luca, the eldest of the three brothers, and his uncle Iorgu, the youngest, also for a time acted in the company of players led by Costache. Luca married the well-known actress Calliopi. But about 1850 he was separated from her and left the stage, becoming secretary to the monastery of Mărgineni not far from Ploeşti in Wallachia. Here he settled down in the local village, Haimanale, with the daughter of a Greek merchant from Braşov (then officially known as Kronstadt) in Transylvania. She was regarded as his wife, though in fact he never divorced Calliopi. And so Ion Luca Caragiale, born on January 30, 1852, and his sister Elena, born three or four years later, were regarded as legitimate.

In this hamlet of Haimanale by the monastery the infant Caragiale spent his early years. When the time came for his primary schooling he was sent to Ploeşti, which was not yet the great oil-refining center but a country town. In later years Caragiale was inclined to pose as a self-educated man who had been through only four years of primary education, but in fact he continued at Ploeşti at a "gymnasium" (high school) until he was fifteen. He was then sent with his mother and sister to Bucharest to attend the training course for actors given by his uncle Costache at the Conservatoire. It is likely that this was a concession obtained by the young Caragiale from his father in spite of the latter's own ideas of what his son's career should be. The boy did not, in fact, distinguish himself; he was handicapped by the quality of his voice. His father, who became deputy judge in the county court at Ploeşti, obtained for him a post as copyist in the court in the summer of 1870. This he did not hold for long. In autumn his father died, and he soon returned to Bucharest, where he presently became prompter and copyist at the National Theater. He was now the breadwinner for his mother and sister as well as himself; so to increase his income he took on the task of proofreading for two newspapers.

He was to say in later years that he had had sufficient preliminary training to have been able to go in for the law and thus to have made himself a successful legal or political career, but that he had not done so because from his days at primary school he had felt a vocation for literature.[1] He did not publish until the age of twenty-one, when contributions signed "Car" or "Palicar" began to appear in the weekly periodical *Ghimpele* (The Thorn). After a few numbers it expired. In 1877 he brought out a humorous weekly in miniature format called *Claponul* (The Capon). In 1877 the Russo-Turkish War broke out, the war from which the United Principalities (as Wallachia and Moldavia had become in 1859) gained their independence of Turkey and became the kingdom of Romania, with Karl of Hohenzollern-Sigmaringen (their prince since 1867) as King Carol I. On the outbreak of war Frédéric Damé, a Frenchman who had settled in Bucharest, proposed to Caragiale that they should together produce a nonpolitical paper of war news. They decided to call it *Naţiunea română* (The Romanian Nation). For the seven days which it lasted it was very successful; then, by an unfortunate error having announced the capture of Plevna by King Carol's army, it was suppressed by the government for spreading false news. Caragiale then did dramatic criticisms for *România liberă* (Free Romania). Here it seems that his attacks on the venality of critics and the plagiarism of playwrights lost him his job after a few weeks. He next contributed political articles to the Conservative paper *Timpul* (Time), which was edited by the poet Eminescu.

But he was now on the eve of a success which was to change the direction of his activities for the next decade. His translation of a French verse tragedy *Rome Vaincue* by Al. Parodi was produced at the National Theater in Bucharest on May 21, 1878, and was warmly received. Five days later he made his first appearance at the famous literary circle *Junimea* (Youth), presided over by Titu Maiorescu. In November, when *Junimea* held its annual banquet in Jassy, the town where the circle had originally been formed, Caragiale read a play of his own before that convivial but critical audience. This comedy was *O noapte furtunoasă* (A Stormy Night). The reading made a great impression. But the first performance on January 18, 1879, at the National Theater was not altogether well received. Damé in his criticism advised parents not to let their daughters see it. At the second performance the Director of the theater, Ion Ghica, cut out a scene which was capable of giving offense. Caragiale, furious, entered the director's office and, receiving no satisfaction, exploded into insults. The play was not presented again. Because Maiorescu helped Caragiale to draft letters to Ghica and others concerned, the play when printed in *Convorbiri literare* (Literary Conversations), the organ of *Junimea,* was dedicated by the grateful author to Maiorescu. Thanks to the same benefactor, Caragiale had his first trip abroad, accompanying the Maiorescus to Vienna.

The farce *Conul Leonida faţă cu reacţiunea* (Mr. Leonida faced with Reaction) was printed in *Convorbiri literare* of February, 1880. Clearly Ion Ghica was not going to accept it for the National Theater after his brush with the author over *O noapte furtunoasă*. It was evidently performed elsewhere, because Maiorescu in 1885 made a note that it had been put on at a second-rate theater and was not a success. But it was not presented at the National Theater until 1912, the year of Caragiale's death.

His conditions of service with the Conservative paper *Timpul* were miserable, and his connection with it ended in 1881. In the autumn he was appointed inspector of schools in the districts of Suceava and Neamţu in the north of Moldavia. It was during this winter in Moldavia that he had an affair with the poetess Veronica Micle, beloved by Eminescu, thus wrecking his friendship with the poet. In the following February Caragiale was moved to the Argeş-Vîlcea district in Wallachia. On February 18 the National Theater, which was no longer under the directorship of Ion Ghica, produced the farce *Soacra mea Fifina*, which was later printed under the title *O soacră* (A Mother-in-law).

A year later Caragiale resigned his inspectorship. Iacob Negruzzi, a founder member of Junimea and editor of *Convorbiri literare*, offered him the post of stage director at the National Theater in Jassy, of which he was himself director, but Caragiale refused. Negruzzi and he then collaborated on the text of an operetta based on N. Gane's story *Hatmanul Baltag* with music by Eduard Caudella. This was performed at the National Theater, Bucharest, on March 1, 1884.

It would not have been surprising if the public had felt that Caragiale's dramatic production since 1880 was disappointing. He was now, however, on the eve of a great success. On October 24 at *Junimea's* annual gathering at Jassy he read his new comedy, *O scrisoare pierdută* (A Lost Letter). This was to be staged at the National Theater in Bucharest on November 13. On the previous evening Caragiale was taken by Maiorescu to the royal palace to read his play to the queen (Elizabeth of Wied, who herself under the pen name of "Carmen Sylva," wrote prolifically in German). Next evening she attended the premiere and led the applause. So successful was the play that it had what was then the extraordinary number of eleven consecutive performances. Caragiale was encouraged by his success to resign from a modest post which he had in a tobacco factory.

The tobacco factory had, however, introduced a new complication into his life. One of the women working there had become his mistress and gave birth to a son on March 12, 1885. Caragiale registered the birth, presumably intending at the time to marry the mother and legitimize the son. This was never done. The strained relations between Matei Caragiale and his father were largely due to the grievance of illegitimacy.

Meanwhile, the playwright had been working on another play for a competition instituted by the National Theater. It was called *D'ale carnavalului* (Carnival Doings) and was described as a comedy, though it is more of a farce. At the first night Queen Elizabeth was present, but when she left halfway through, hissing broke out led by an organized claque. Critical comment was unfavorable. The play was printed in *Convorbiri literare* for May, 1885.

In November 1885 there died a wealthy widow, cousin of Caragiale's mother, who inherited a part of her vast estate. Though lawsuits concerning the inheritance dragged on for a quarter of a century, money brought some immediate relief to the family. Caragiale's mother and sister were no longer entirely dependent on him. He gave up work which he had been doing for some months for the Liberal paper *Voinţa naţională* (The National Will).

Maiorescu and some of his fellow Junimists were by now not merely a literary circle, but a political group with hopes of forming a government. If they came to power, Caragiale might hope to benefit from their patronage. In the spring of 1888 the Liberal government which had been in power for twelve years was replaced by a Conservative government dominated by members of *Junimea.* Maiorescu received the Ministry of Education. This seemed to provide a chance for Caragiale to realize his long-cherished dream of being director general of the theaters (i.e., of the National Theater at Bucharest). Nevertheless, Maiorescu did not believe him to have the necessary administrative qualities, nor did Negruzzi. Eventually, however, the previous director was squeezed out by means of an administrative inquiry, and Caragiale appointed in his place.

It was not long before the new director took a step which revealed a characteristic defect of his personality: irritability leading to impulsive and ill-considered actions and to a flouting of good taste. Goaded by unfavorable comments upon his appointment both in the press and still more in the talk of the town, he sent an open letter to the editors of the Bucharest press, stating his qualifications and his intentions as director general of the theaters. But he did not confine himself to these points; he attacked his predecessor in strong terms. Nor was his stress on the appreciation which he enjoyed among the members of *Junimea* likely to conciliate opinion. The letter was not publicized by the press. Nor was the season at the National Theater the success which might have been expected from a director with the background and varied experience of the theater which Caragiale possessed. What was perhaps his most satisfying achievement of the season came in the middle of it: in the course of duty at the front of the house he met Alexandrina Burelly, daughter of an architect, fell in love with her, and was married. Three months after returning from his honeymoon in Italy he resigned his post. In the same month, May, his comedies were printed with a critical preface by Maiorescu.

Caragiale must already have set his mind to the writing of stories and sketches which was to be the principal activity of the remainder of his literary career, though he had not yet quite finished with the drama. His story "O făclie de Paşte" (An Easter Candle) appeared in *Convorbiri literare* for August, 1889. In June he had already started to contribute articles to the Junimist paper *Constituţionalul* (The Constitutionalist). Here in June appeared his fine tribute to Eminescu, *In Nirvana.* These contributions ended in the autumn. Perhaps Caragiale for the moment felt himself a man of means, since after his mother's death in 1888, he was heir to half her estate. He must have been writing his tragic drama *Năpasta* (False Witness),[2] for in December it was finished and he read it to the Maiorescus and Negruzzi. It was printed in *Convorbiri literare* for January, 1890, with a dedication to Mrs. Maiorescu. The first performance was at the National Theater in Bucharest on February 3, 1890; the public received it coldly. Later it was printed in book form. Caragiale then put forward this volume and the one containing his comedies for the Eliade Rădulescu prize offered by the Romanian Academy. At a session of the academy held on April 14, 1892, B. P. Haşdeu, philologist and author, gave an unfavorable report, and although Iacob Negruzzi spoke up in defense of the plays, they were rejected by twenty votes to three.

Caragiale's connection with Maiorescu was coming to an end. It seems that he was disappointed that the minister had never offered him as good a post as he would have liked. The break came in 1892, when Caragiale delivered a public lecture attacking *Junimea* as a literary and as a political clique and then included in a volume of *Note şi schiţe* (Notes and Sketches), mostly reprinted from periodicals, a note taking

Maiorescu to task in remarkably violent terms for altering the text of Eminescu's poems in his posthumous edition. So ended his connection with Maiorescu, who years later refused a reconciliation; nor did Caragiale ever again contribute to *Convorbiri literare.*

In the same year *O făclie de Paşte* appeared in a booklet with two new stories, "Păcat" (Sin) and "Om cu noroc" (Lucky Man). The winter brought domestic tragedy: the Caragiales lost their two little girls (aged one and one-half years and two months, respectively). However, a son Luca was born in the summer. Caragiale now started a humorous periodical, *Moftul român* (Romanian Nonsense), to which he contributed sketches; it had no particular political slant. After a few months *Moftul român* ceased publication. Despite his inheritance, Caragiale was not a man of independent means. He now took a share in opening a beer hall in Bucharest, the first of several ventures of this kind. The poet and critic Macedonski, whom he had often attacked, wrote an article deploring the government's indifference to literary talent, which reduced the writer to such expedients. Once more in 1894 Caragiale took part in a journalistic venture, joining the Transylvanian Romanians Slavici and Coşbuc in the production of a family magazine *Vatra* (The Hearth). As might have been expected, this was not the sort of journal to fit Caragiale's gifts, and he soon withdrew. It was in this year that his daughter Ecaterina was born.

His life from 1895 to 1901 was uneventful. He enrolled in September, 1895, in the Radical party led by G. Panu and in 1896 followed its leader into the Conservative party. In that year he made an attempt to get himself appointed director of the National Theater in Jassy, but without success. From 1899 to 1901 he held a post in the Office of the State Monopolies. When he was dismissed on grounds of economy, he started a second series of *Moftul român*, which ran for some six months and also tried his hand again as a beer-hall proprietor. The year 1901 was a trying one for him, although at its start his friends had given him a banquet to celebrate his twenty-five years of literary activity. In two articles in *Revista literară* a certain C. A. Ionescu using the pen name "Caion" accused him of plagiarism in his drama *Năpasta*. The accusation was quite unfounded; Caion had invented an imaginary Hungarian playwright as the author whose work was supposedly plagiarized. In December Caragiale brought a lawsuit. Yet in January Caion made another allegation in an article published in Macedonski's periodical *Forţa morală* (Moral Force); this time he claimed that *O scrisoare pierdută* was plagiarized from Sardou's play *Rabagas.* And next month an unsigned note in *Forţa morală* claimed that *D'ale carnavalului* was copied from *Le Carnaval d'un Merle Blanc* of Chivot and Duru. It is clear that Macedonski could not forgive Caragiale for the parodies of his symbolist poetry written by Caragiale and published in the second series of *Moftul român.* The libel action was heard in March. Caragiale's friend Barbu Delavrancea led for the prosecution, and Caion was condemned in his absence to three months' imprisonment with a fine and costs.

But trouble was ahead. On March 23, a committee of the Romanian Academy met to award the Năsturel-Herescu prize. Among the entries was Caragiale's *Momente,* a volume of stories and sketches which he had collected in 1901 and which included the masterly "La hanul lui Mînjoală" (At Mînjoală's Inn). In spite of the report in favor by D. C. Ollănescu, *Momente* was rejected by five votes to two, and the prize was awarded to a collection of historical documents. Then in June an appeal by Caion was heard before a different jury, and he was acquitted.

The events of 1902 must have made Caragiale feel very bitter. He began to consider leaving Romania. Once before, in 1892, he had thought of moving to Transylvania. But the Austro-Hungarian authorities were likely to be very suspicious of a famous Romanian writer from the Kingdom of Romania coming to settle in Transylvania. Eventually in 1905, being temporarily affluent, he took his wife and children abroad, to Austria, Italy, Switzerland, France, Holland, and Germany. Returning to Bucharest after a year of touring, he decided that they would move for good to Berlin. The choice, as his daughter says, is hard to understand in view of his temperament. She attributes it largely to her father's anxiety for his children's health, an exaggerated anxiety which seems uncharacteristic, indeed inexplicable until we remember that he had lost two children by an infectious disease. Hence the appeal of the temperate climate and cleanliness of Berlin. She believes that his love of classical music also helped to determine his choice.[3]

He frequently visited Romania, and he contributed to Romanian periodicals. In 1905 he started to work on a comedy which was to present characters from *O noapte furtunoasă* and *O scrisoare pierdută* in the social status which they had attained after a quarter of a century. For this play–*Titircă, Sotirescu et C-ie*, as it was to be called–Caragiale never got beyond lists of characters and a very brief outline. The only theatrical work he achieved was a slight occasional piece called

Incepem! (We're Starting!)–it is about a rehearsal–which was produced for one night in 1909. The peasant revolt in Romania in 1907 inspired him to write articles which were printed in pamphlet form as *1907, Din primăvară în toamnă* (1907, From Spring to Autumn) and which sold over ten thousand copies. The tale of *Kir Ianulea,* one of his finest works, appeared in 1909. For his sixtieth birthday in 1912 friends in Romania wished to organize a jubilee, but he refused. In the spring he had the pleasure of seeing a series of remarkable poems by Matei (the illegitimate son, with whom his relationship was often tense) published in *Viaţa românească* (Romanian Life). It was with his other son Luca that he spent the night of July 8/9, 1912, in an unusual outpouring of recollections and confidences. Next day he was found dead by his bed, struck down by arteriosclerosis.

CHAPTER 2

Comedies before 1884

THE theatrical success which in 1878 was the prelude to a decade of playwriting by Caragiale, was a translation, not an original work, and a translation of a play in a genre which, in his original work, he was never to attempt, namely, tragedy in verse. *Roma învinsă* is from the five-act tragedy *Rome vaincue* of Alexandre Parodi. It is set in the Rome of the Second Punic War, when the city is in danger after Hannibal's victory at Cannae. The tragedy is that of a Vestal Virgin, Opimia, whose love affair with Lentulus has brought the wrath of the gods upon Rome and who has to expiate her sacrilege by death. Caragiale, never a poet, was in fact a fluent versifier, and his version is skilful and convincing. It antedates Vasile Alecsandri's verse dramas.

Five days after the premiere of *Roma învinsă* Caragiale made his first appearance at *Junimea* which, now that Titu Maiorescu and others of its leading figures were established in Bucharest, held its regular meetings in that city. Caragiale's debut in the literary circle may be connected with his recent success, as Maiorescu in his diary notes the presence of Caragiale, adding the description "good translator of Parodi's *Rome Conquered.*"[1] This was the last meeting of the season. In the following November *Junimea* held its annual dinner at Jassy, its original home. Before the dinner Caragiale gave a reading of his first original play *O noapte furtunoasă*.[2]

I O noapte furtunoasă

The scene of *O noapte furtunoasă* is the house of Dumitrache, a timber merchant and captain in the Civic Guard, at Bucharest. The curtain rises on Dumitrache complaining to his friend Ipingescu, a police subcommissar, that when he had taken his wife Veta and her divorced sister Ziţa to an open-air cabaret, an unknown person, by the look of him a clerk, had made eyes at the ladies and had followed them part of the way home. A week later Ziţa had pressed for another visit to the cabaret, and the same thing had happened again. Dumitrache had intended to teach the unknown a lesson, after seeing the ladies safely indoors, but the man had escaped. At this point the voice of Chiriac, Dumitrache's assistant in the timber business and sergeant in the Civic Guard, is heard outside; Ipingescu suggests that he ought not to hear this conversation. Dumitrache protests his entire confidence in his assistant. Chiriac then comes in, reports his activities as sergeant, and reminds Dumitrache that he is duty captain tonight. The apprentice Spiridon arrives with the newspaper. Left alone again with Dumitrache, Ipingescu reads aloud to him a bombastic political article signed "R. Vent . . . ," of which Dumitrache expresses approval. At a noise from outside–which is, in fact, Ziţa quarreling with her former husband–they rush out.

Spiridon, re-entering, soliloquizes on his unjust treatment by his master, until Ziţa comes in. He gives her a love letter and says that its writer is waiting outside. When Veta comes out of the next room, Ziţa asks her to let Spiridon fetch something from her house. She has, however, really given him a message to the writer of the letter to wait for her. When Spiridon has gone, Ziţa re-enacts to Veta the scene which she has just had with her former husband. She goes off in tears because Veta turns down her suggestion of another visit to the cabaret. When Spiridon comes back, Veta asks him where Chiriac is. After he has told her what an ill humor Chiriac is in, she sends him to bed. Presently Chiriac enters. Veta and he are ill at ease. As the dialogue proceeds, it becomes clear that they have been lovers till yesterday, when they quarreled because Chiriac believed that there was something between Veta and the man who followed her party home. Chiriac hints at suicide and draws his bayonet. Veta struggles with him, and they are reconciled. As he embraces her, Dumitrache's voice is heard outside calling for Chiriac. From the window Chiriac calls reassuringly back, and as Dumitrache continues on his rounds, the curtain falls on Chiriac renewing the embrace.

As Act II opens, Chiriac and Veta are parting for the night. When he has gone out, she turns the lamp down and prepares for bed. In the dim light the door opens, and there enters Rică Venturiano, the "clerk" who followed the party home from the cabaret (and who in fact is the journalist who wrote the article read aloud by Ipingescu). He addresses Veta ardently, under the impression that she is Ziţa. Scared, Veta screams for help, but as he explains himself, she realizes his mistake and turns up the light. She warns him to avoid being found by her husband. Dumitrache's voice is heard outside. Veta tells Rică to escape through the window onto scaffolding. Dumitrache and Ipingescu burst in to find him; his spectacles and top hat had been visible through the window. Veta is sent to her room, and Spiridon and Chiriac are awakened to join in the search. As Chiriac makes for the window, Veta returns and tries to stop him, but he persists. When the men have gone, Ziţa appears, having been warned by Spiridon. Veta tells her that Rică has escaped along the scaffolding; but Ziţa reveals that the back gate is locked. At the sound of a gunshot both hasten off.

RICĂ *(comes down slowly through the window by which he left. He is covered with whitewash, cement and brick dust; his hair is in disorder; his hat torn; his face is yellow and drawn; he is trembling and his tongue gets tangled up when he speaks; he imagines things in his panic and is weak at the joints)* I'm safe so far! St. Andrew, keep me safe from now on; I'm still a youth! Good genius of Romania's future, protect me; I too am a Romanian! *(pants and presses his pounding heart)* Oh, what a stormy night! A horrible tragedy! *(he fancies he hears something and trembles)* What adventures! I got out of the window and felt my way along the planks. I kept well in to the wall and reached the end of the scaffolding. Destiny persecutes me implacably! The scaffolding was a dead end; there was no ladder. That treacherous lady had misled me. I try to return, and suddenly I hear the enemy coming toward me along the planks. I turn back again without knowing where I'm going; I stumble over a barrel of cement. An inspiration—as a poet I constantly have inspirations!—I hide in the barrel! The steps of the enemy are approaching at speed, a large number of people pass quickly by my barrel, cursing me; being an educated youth, I pretend not to hear. They all go away. I hear a noise, shouts, women's screams, finally a shot. Then the noise slowly fades, all remains in lugubrious silence, only from afar the clock of the Institute is heard striking twenty past eleven . . . an hour of doom for me! I emerge quietly from my barrel, crawl on all fours along the planks, and find myself back here. What am I to do? Which is the way out? I need an ingenious inspiration . . . *(puts his hand to his forehead and thinks)* Got it! Go out through the door *(goes quickly to the door upstage and opens it; outside in the hall it is pitch dark)* Absolute obscurity! *(goes to the window)* Ah! I hear steps; someone is coming along the planks *(hastens R. to the door of Spiridon's room)* This way! *(Spiridon enters swiftly at the same moment, and they collide chest to chest)* Oh, how you scared me! *(comes over dizzy)*

SP. You still here, sir? Things are very hot; you must run for it. If they lay hands on you, they'll kill you.
RI. Kill me? Save me, my boy, get me out of here. Which way out? *(making for the door R., by which Spiridon entered)* This way. . . .
SP. Can't be done! *(bars his way)* The room through here comes out on the main stairs; do you want to meet them face to face?
RI. No, I don't, but what's to be done? My existence is imperiled. I want to get away. Get me away. I'll tip you three quarters of a rouble.
SP. Three quarters of a rouble! Six packets of tobacco! I'll save you.
RI. How? Which way? Tell me quick; I'm in a hurry, I'm in a tight corner.
SP. You stay here. I'll go into that room *(points R.)*, open the door which gives on to the stairs, and when I see them going up, I'll call you in, we'll close the door between, and when they all get in here, I'll let you out at the far side on to the stairs. You'll go down and get quickly out of the gate. Never mind, I'll save you, don't worry.
RI. Yes, go quickly.
SP. *(slyly)* But aren't you going to give me it?
RI. What?
SP. What you promised.
RI. Oh yes, of course! *(looks in all his pockets and makes up the sum from small change; Spiridon counts it greedily)* My boy! *(solemnly)* Young man! Do you realize in what a position I find myself! Do you know what peril threatens me?
SP. You bet I do. Don't I know master's beatings? Never mind, if you don't succeed in escaping . . .
RI. Eh? *(dithers)*
SP. You'll see what a tartar he is . . . why he's called "old Bilious."
RI. No, I don't want to see. Get me out of here.
SP. *(rather coldly)* Oh, of course, if I can, I'll save you, naturally.
RI. Ah! *(dithers)* I hear a noise on the stairs; they're going up. *(dithers)* Hurry; save me! *(Spiridon slowly goes off R., counting the coins; Rică hastens him from behind)*
RI. *(alone for a moment; mime; suddenly steps are heard from the room R., and Spiridon yelling)* Ah! *(steps on the stairs; Rică rushes to door R.)*
DUMITRACHE *(meeting him with drawn sword)* Halt!
RI. *(recoiling)* St. Andrew, I'm done for! *(dashes to the window L. where the scaffolding is)*
CHIRIAC *(meeting him, jumps through the window onto the stage with bayonet fixed as for a charge)* Halt!
RI. *(recoiling in a dither)* Good genius of Romania's future! *(dashes to the door upstage)*
IPINGESCU *(meeting him with drawn sword)* Halt!

Ipingescu, however, recognizes him and vouches for his respectability. When Dumitrache hears that Rică is the author of the article, he is much impressed and readily agrees to his marriage with Ziţa. The only thing that worries Dumitrache is that on his wife's bed he has found a neckcloth. But when Chiriac claims it as his, the jealous husband's suspicions vanish.

The main theme of *O noapte furtunoasă* had already appeared in outline in a little piece which Caragiale printed in his comic periodical *Claponul* two years before.[3] In this, Ghiţă Calup, a grocer and member of the Civic Guard, has an assistant called Ilie, of whom he is very fond and to whom he makes a birthday present of a neckcloth. He is very jealous of his wife's honor, and whenever he has to go on guard duty, urges Ilie to watch over her, adding that he intends to make him his partner. Returning once unexpectedly early, he is let in by a sleepy Ilie and finds the crumpled neckcloth on his bed. Next morning he blames his assistant for not looking after his birthday present properly! "Thenceforth," comments Caragiale, "Ilie was a *partner,* the degree of partnership depending on the amount of guard duty that fell to his master's lot."

This theme of the deceived husband, unshakably confident in the good faith of a younger assistant who is in fact his wife's lover, was to recur in *O scrisoare pierdută*, where the triangle Trahanache–Zoe–Tipătescu corresponds to the one here formed by Dumitrache–Veta–Chiriac. In the later play the theme is transposed; the social position and background of the triangle is much superior to that in *O noapte furtunoasă*. The repellent faults of Dumitrache–his jealousy and his ill treatment of Spiridon–have no counterpart in the more amiable Trahanache. And Dumitrache's political views are quite different: he is fascinated by the liberal ideas and verbiage of Rică Venturiano. Less sophisticated than Trahanache, he utters more malapropisms.

As for the interwoven theme, the intrigue of Rică Venturiano with Ziţa, Caragiale once told his younger friend Paul Zarifopol that Rică's adventure was one that he himself had had.[4]

II Conul Leonida faţă cu reacţiunea

Maiorescu notes among the readings at *Junimea* in the autumn season of 1879 Caragiale's "little farce" *Conul Leonida faţă cu reacţiunea.*[5] The piece was printed in *Convorbiri literare* for February, 1880. When and where it was first staged is not known; Maiorescu states that it was played in a second-rate theater and did not please.[6] It is a one-act farce with only three characters. Leonida, a pensioner aged sixty, and his wife Efimiţa, are sitting in their room ready for bed. He is describing the excitement in Bucharest fourteen years before at the overthrow of Prince Cuza. The couple go to bed, and he tells her what the benefits of a republic would be. Very soon after they have gone to sleep, shots and shouting are heard outside. Efimiţa wakes up and rouses Leonida. As the noise has ceased, he supposes that she has been dreaming; he calms her, and they go to bed again. Once more they are roused by the noise. Leonida says it cannot be a revolution, as the Liberals are in power; then, looking at his Liberal newspaper, he sees a warning against the forces of reaction. Scared by the danger he is in as a known republican, he and Efimiţa barricade the door against the supposed reactionaries. No sooner have they done so than knocking begins. As the shots and shouting fade away into the distance, they realize that the person knocking at the door is their own daily servant, Safta, come to light the fire early. When admitted, she explains that there has been an uproarious party nearby and that the noise was due to revelers going home.

The world here depicted overlaps with that of *O noapte furtunoasă*; indeed, it is Dumitrache's crony, the police subcommissar Nae Ipingescu who, in drunken exuberance, fires the shots that scare Leonida. But although the two plays deal with the same society, *Conul Leonida* has less universality. In comparison with *O noapte furtunoasă* its appeal is more purely local and topical. The fun depends chiefly on the satirical depiction of a naïve "progressive," who has swallowed the verbiage of Liberal demagogues without digesting any ideas, and on the malapropisms uttered by himself and his wife. In *O noapte furtunoasă* these elements are balanced by others of more universal appeal. This is not to deny that *Conul Leonida* is successful in its own genre of farcical curtain-raiser.

Probably the reason why *Conul Leonida* was not produced at the National Theater was not so much its own deserts as the quarrel between Caragiale and the director, Ion Ghica. We may infer this from the fact that after a change of director the National Theater accepted an inferior farce by Caragiale, which was produced under the title of *Soacra mea Fifina*. (When printed, it was entitled *O soacră*.) The scene is "a Grand Hotel in Bucharest." Holding an extravagantly idealistic view of love, Fifina, stepmother of Iulia, has only consented to Iulia's marriage with Alexandru Peruzeanu on condition that during the first three months of the marriage, she, Fifina, is in absolute control.

Accordingly, she is staying with the couple on their honeymoon and preventing them ever being alone together. Peruzeanu in despair comes back to the hotel with a sleeping powder of which he intends to administer an overdose to Fifina in place of the quinine which she commissioned him to buy. He finds the chambermaid Liza in tears because her fiancé Victor, a waiter, is distracted and does not do his work. (He is, in fact, fascinated by Fifina.) Peruzeanu promises to help Liza. He tries to encourage Victor by saying that he knows all about his love and assuring him that "she" loves him. Victor thinks that the "she" in question is Fifina. Peruzeanu administers a sleeping dose to Fifina, who tells him how she came to marry Iulia's elderly father instead of a young man who loved her. She goes back to her room. From another room emerges Furtunescu, a former friend of Peruzeanu, who has been serving for years in the British army. Peruzeanu discovers that Furtunescu is Fifina's former sweetheart. When Fifina comes out of her room, she is met by Victor, who declares his passion by reading out speeches from a novelette. Furtunescu, coming in, pushes him aside and embraces Fifina. Peruzeanu discovers that the chemist had after all given him quinine, so that Fifina is in no danger. The couples are thus enabled to pair off.

The social atmosphere of *O soacră* is quite different from that of the preceding plays. All the characters except the waiter and the chambermaid are from the professional class. Caragiale's imagination was not fired, and the piece has the cold, dead unreality of, let us say, a comedy by W. S. Gilbert. When Peruzeanu soliloquizes at great length or Fifina tells the story of her love, there is neither idiosyncrasy of style to bring out character nor any attempt at parody. Caragiale in 1898 made a list of his dramatic works in chronological order of composition, putting *O soacră* first with the date of 1876. It has been pointed out that the list has clear errors (or misrepresentations), as for instance the dating of *Conul Leonida* to 1880 when we know that Caragiale read it to *Junimea* in the autumn of 1879. It has therefore been suggested that he antedated the composition of *O soacră* to excuse its inferior quality.[7] Nevertheless, it may be that he did write it in 1876 and, having laid it aside, produced it when he had no new play ready for the stage. It may, in fact, be a first attempt at playwriting before he had found his true vein.

III Hatmanul Baltag

O soacră was first presented on February 17, 1883. A year later (March 1, 1884) the National Theater staged the operetta *Hatmanul*

Baltag, libretto by Caragiale and Iacob Negruzzi, music by Eduard Caudella. It is based on a short story of the same name by the Moldavian writer N. Gane, printed in *Convorbiri literare*, August, 1874. Gane described his story in a footnote as an "imitation of Dickens." It is in tone very much the sort of story which Dickens puts into the mouth of characters in *The Pickwick Papers*, and the theme is reminiscent of Scrooge's encounter with the ghost of Marley in *A Christmas Carol*. Hatmanul Baltag is a Moldavian boyar devoted to hunting and drinking with his cronies. Growing bored, he decides to marry. His wife soon shows her determination to run the household and makes him dismiss his cronies. And so in middle age he finds himself harassed by a large family of children, by his talkative mother-in-law, and by debt. Contemplating suicide, he retires with a jug of wine and his pipe for a last solace. Presently he notices a hideous figure by the fireside. It is the Spirit of Suicide waiting for him to kill himself. Baltag concludes from the ensuing conversation that he will not gain by doing so, and as his spirits rise, his laughter drives the Spirit away. So Baltag speaks his mind to his womenfolk and sets his house in order.

The operetta is so different from the story that it might be described in modern phraseology as "from an idea by N. Gane." In the story Baltag was the only character portrayed at any length. In the libretto other characters have to be developed and new ones introduced. The most drastic changes are the introduction of Stacan, a boon companion of Baltag, and the transformation of the mother-in-law into the bride's aunt, Arghiriţa, an old flame of Stacan. The scene is Moldavia in the Middle Ages. The action is divided into five tableaux. The first takes place in a mountain landscape; Baltag, Stacan, and the cronies set off hunting. Then a messenger, Sotir, brings in a letter from Baltag to Zulnia, the girl he proposes to marry. It is read by Arghiriţa; she and Zulnia sing of love as each sees it. In the second tableau the hunters return to carouse in the wine cellar; Baltag announces his intention to marry and is derided by Stacan and the rest. The third tableau is the wedding feast; Stacan recognizes Arghiriţa and pursues her so ardently that he has to leave in disgrace. The fourth tableau takes place years later; Stacan in disguise and under the protection of Arghiriţa is acting as private tutor to the numerous children of Baltag. Baltag, desperate with the humiliations of his family life, dresses as a warrior and goes off mysteriously. In the final tableau, down in the cellar, Baltag recalls his happy days and is about to throw himself on his blade when Stacan appears, pretending to be his own ghost. He persuades Baltag that life in the next world lacks the wine and merriment of this one. Then Baltag asserts himself, and all ends happily.

Obviously a libretto is difficult to judge in separation from its musical setting. The comedies of W. S. Gilbert have above been mentioned disparagingly. If we now compare his libretti for the Gilbert and Sullivan operettas with that of *Hatmanul Baltag* (produced in the same year as *Princess Ida* and a year before *The Mikado*) and note the relative absence of wit in the Romanian libretto, we must remember that the public for such an operetta in Bucharest was much less sophisticated than that which frequented the "Savoy operas." Even so, it is surprising that Caragiale's comic invention is limited to some deliberate anachronisms, such as the post-office terminology put into the mouth of Sotir when he brings Baltag's letter to his future bride, the educational jargon uttered by Stacan in his pose as a schoolmaster, and Baltag's explanation of his dressing up that he is "going to the photographer's."

It is not clear what contribution each of the collaborators made to the libretto. In a letter to the director general of the National Theater, Caragiale renounced any share in the royalties on the ground that his contribution was minimal. Negruzzi records that Caragiale had proposed collaboration on a comic opera, but after they had chosen the subject, was slow to get to work. "Caragiale did the prose, I the verses and we did the adaptation [*înscenarea*] together."[8] Caragiale had made the original proposals to the National Theater in his own name, and it has been suggested that no mention was made of Negruzzi before they were accepted because Negruzzi did not want to risk being exposed to a setback in public. It may be that even if Caragiale first suggested the collaboration, he really took only a small part in writing the libretto.

CHAPTER 3

Comedies: 1884, O scrisoare pierdută

THE same year, 1884, was to see the culmination of Caragiale's career as a playwright. There is some evidence that he had had *O scrisoare pierdută* in mind for several years; in the autumn of 1884 he was busy finishing it. On September 23 he read it to *Junimea* in Bucharest, and on October 26 read it again at the *Junimea* anniversary banquet in Jassy.[1] The first performance was at the National Theater at Bucharest on November 13 in the presence of the queen and with a full house. The play was well received and ran for thirteen nights, an unusually long run for that time and place. In the following month productions were staged in Jassy and Craiova. *O scrisoare pierdută* was printed in the February and March issues of *Convorbiri literare* in 1885.

The setting of the comedy is a county town in the mountains. The curtain rises on an antechamber in the house of Ştefan Tipătescu, the prefect of the county. Ghiţă Pristanda, the police chief, tells him how during the night he listened at an open window at the house of Nae Caţavencu, the editor of the local newspaper belonging to the political party in opposition. He overheard Caţavencu say to his political associates that Tipătescu would find that someone on whose vote he counted without question would vote instead for the opposition. Caţavencu was just about to read out a letter when the company was startled by a noise and shut the window. This report puzzles Tipătescu, who tells Ghiţă to follow up the matter and then goes off to change before lunching at the house of Zaharia Trahanache, chairman of the local electoral committee. Trahanache enters in a state of excitement. Tipătescu comes back, and Ghiţă is sent off to tell Zoe, Trahanache's wife, that the two men will be late for lunch. But at that moment Zoe puts her head through another door and signals to Ghiţă to join her. Trahanache is left alone with Tipătescu.

TIP. Well, Zaharia, old man, what is it? Tell me. You look rather changed.

TR. Just a moment. You'll see. This morning about half past eight my manservant comes into my room—I'd not even drunk my coffee—and gives me a note and tells me they're waiting for an answer. . . . Now, who was the note from?
TIP. Well, who?
TR. From Mr. Nae Caţavencu.
TIP. Caţavencu?
TR. I said to myself: "What has Caţavencu to do with me, or I with Caţavencu? We've nothing in common; in fact, to judge by principles, quite the reverse."
TIP. Of course. Well?
TR. Wait, you'll see. (*takes a note from his pocket and gives it to Tipătescu*)
TIP. (*taking the note and reading*) "To the Honorable Mr. Trahanache, Chairman of the Permanent Committee, of the Schools Committee, of the Electoral Committee, of the Agricultural Committee and of other committees. By Hand" (*taking the letter from the envelope*) "Dear Sir, In the interests of your honor as a citizen and father of a family, we beg you to call today between 9:30 and 10:00 A.M. at the office of the newspaper 'The Roar of the Carpathians' and premises of the Encyclopedic-Cooperative Society 'Romanian Economic Dawn,' where you will be shown a document of the highest importance to yourself. Yours faithfully, Caţavencu, Founder-Chairman of the Encyclopedic-Cooperative Society 'Romanian Economic Dawn.' " Well? What document?
TR. Just a moment. You'll see. I thought: shall I go, shan't I? Well, just out of curiosity I'll go to see what this nonsense is about. I dressed quickly, Fănică, and off I went.
TIP. To Caţavencu?
TR. Wait, you'll see. Yes, to Caţavencu. When I go in, he gets up respectfully and offers me a chair. "My dear sir" this and "My dear sir" that. "I'm sorry there's been this coolness between us," says he; "I've always thought a great deal of you as the leading figure in our county"—and, in short, a heap of flattering remarks. I tell him straight: "Sir, you sent for me to show me a document; show it to me!" He says: "I'm afraid," says he, "that it will be a cruel blow for you, and I ought to have prepared you in advance. You, a man of such . . ." and more flattery. I say again: "Just a moment, sir; the document!" "Well," says he, the ladies . . ." Just see where the scoundrel was leading me! Poor Zoe! Don't say a word to her, in case she finds out! She's so sensitive!
TIP. What! Did he dare? The swine! (*rises excitedly*)
TR. (*stopping him*) Wait, you'll see! "Well," he says, "the ladies don't always realize a husband's merits and moral qualities and the respect

which, in a word, they ought to feel for him." In short (*Tipătescu is very excited*), why should I go on spinning it out? As soon as I put my foot down and say "Now listen, sir, just a moment; the document!," the scoundrel sees that he has no choice and gives me a letter. Guess who it was from and who to?
TIP. (*scarcely controlling his excitement*) Who was it from, Zaharia?
TR. Wait, you'll see! (*bluntly and with a laugh*) From you to my wife – to Zoe; a full-blow love letter! Eh? What do you say to that?
TIP. (*extremely upset*) Impossible, impossible!
TR. I've read it ten times, maybe; I know it by heart! Just listen. "My dear Zoe, The Honorable (that's me) is going to the meeting this evening (that's the meeting the night before last). I (that's you) must stay at home, because I'm expecting despatches from Bucharest, to which I must reply by return. Perhaps the Minister may even call me to the telegraph. So don't expect me; *you* must come (that's my wife, Zoe) to your ducky (that's you), who adores you as always, and sends you a thousand kisses. Fănică." (*looks hard at Tipătescu, who is extremely agitated*)
TIP. (*walking up and down in fury*) Impossible! I'll break that swine's bones! Impossible!
TR. (*placidly*) Of course it's impossible! But just fancy such dastardly conduct! (*straightforwardly*) Well, old man, I understand forgery up to a point, but to such a point as this . . . it's beyond me. Look, Fănică, you should see the imitation of your handwriting! You'd say it was your own; you'd swear it, you would indeed! (*stopping and looking at Tipătescu, who is walking about with clenched fists; with surprise and dismay*) Just look how excited he is! Never mind, man, say he's a scoundrel and have done with it! That's life; you can't help it. *We* shan't change it. Who could imagine the lengths that scoundrel would go to?
TIP. (*as before*) That swine!
TR. Just a moment, my dear man. Tell him what I told him: "You're a great one for Machiavellian tricks, sir, a great one, I don't deny it; but you've got the wrong man." When he saw that he was cutting no ice with me, do you know what he stooped to? He tells me that if I attach no importance to it, the public will, for the letter will be published in Sunday's newspaper and will be hung in the window for anyone to inspect who cares to.
TIP. (*raving*) I'll shoot him! I'll burn him alive! They must bring him at once, alive or dead, with that letter! (*rushes upstage*) Ghiţă, Ghiţă! I must see the police officer.

So, fortunately for the prefect, Trahanache takes it for granted that the letter is a forgery. No sooner has he left for home than Zoe appears and shows Tipătescu a note which she has received from Caţavencu, offering to restore the letter if she will influence Tipătescu to support Caţavencu as candidate in the forthcoming parliamentary elections. The scene is interrupted by the arrival of Farfuridi, the presumptive candidate of the government party, with another supporter, Brînzovenescu, their suspicions have been aroused by the comings and goings of Trahanache, his wife, and Ghiţă at Caţavencu's office. Tipătescu, hearing them coming, hides Zoe; when he returns, they tax him with treachery and produce a leaflet which is already being distributed, to the effect that Trahanache and Tipătescu will support Caţavencu's candidature. The prefect gets rid of them; but no sooner has Zoe re-entered than there appears a Drunken Citizen. He explains amid hiccups that he has found a letter from Tipătescu to Zoe, which Caţavencu tried to buy from him. But now when he offers to hand it over to them, he finds that he no longer has it. Caţavencu must have stolen it while he was fuddled. Trahanache then returns and brings down the curtain with the statement that he has caught Caţavencu with another forgery.

At the beginning of Act II, in the same room, Trahanache is conferring with Farfuridi and Brînzovenescu over the list of electors. He indignantly repudiates the suggestion that Tipătescu is treacherously collaborating with Caţavencu, and stalks out. The other two are convinced that there is treachery afoot and go off to denounce it by an anonymous telegram to Bucharest. Ghiţă returns, looking for Zoe because Caţavencu, whom he has arrested, refuses to speak except to her. When she comes in, she sends him to fetch Caţavencu. She is in great agitation because Caţavencu's paper is announcing the publication of the letter next day. When Tipătescu enters, she begs him to support Caţavencu's candidature. He refuses; in growing desperation, she says she will do it herself and get her husband's support too. As she rushes off, he follows; and on the empty stage appears Ghiţă with Caţavencu. While Ghiţă goes to look for Zoe, Tipătescu reappears.

CA. (*aside*) Tipătescu! I should have preferred her!
TIP. (*after standing in door R. with a frown and fists clenched, goes quietly to door up C., taking Caţavencu's measure with his eyes, and stops a moment upstage; aside*) God help me!
CA. (*embarrassed*) My dear sir, excuse me if I seem to be introducing myself thus informally. I must tell you that I have been brought here by your police officer, by order . . . and I wasn't expecting to meet you.

TIP. (*aside*) Impertinence!
CA. I had been told that I was sent for by . . . otherwise I wouldn't have come. In short, if I am here under arrest, I'll stay . . . ; if I'm free – and that's all I ask . . . I'll withdraw at once.
TIP. (*who has been tapping his heel impatiently all the time, comes slowly downstage and says, distinctly and with clenched teeth*) My dear Mr. Caţavencu, I don't see how between men with some claims to good sense there can be room for such pretenses, such refinements of politeness, such careful speeches, when their situation is so clear. I am a man who likes to lay his cards on the table. Allow me to tell you something. Come on, sit down, please! (*offers him a chair: aside*) I must keep my head. How lucky that Zoe is through there!
CA. My dear sir, you like to put your cards on the table. I agree. I like my game to be short . . . short. (*gesture of cutting short*) We can clear up our situation in no time. (*Tipătescu offers him a chair; he lightly rejects it*) No, thank you.
TIP. (*as before*) Come on, please sit down!
CA. (*as before*) No, thank you!
TIP. (*glaring at Caţavencu and growling*) Come on, now!
CA. (*who has drawn back a little, finally gives in and drops helplessly into the chair*) Thank you!
TIP. That's right (*sits down close to him. Caţavencu withdraws a little. Tipătescu moves up; Caţavencu again withdraws; and so on*) So, my dear sir, you–by some means which is not my concern–are in possession of a letter of mine, which might compromise the honor of a family. . . .
CA. (*gesture*) Ah!
TIP. Excuse me if I have offended you. Let me be even shorter. . . . Look, you are a practical man. You possess something which I need, and you know how much I need it. I come and say to you: (*very affably*) my dear sir, what are you asking in exchange for this thing?
CA. (*innocently*) What? You don't know?
TIP. (*similarly*) No.
CA. (*similarly*) You can't even guess?
TIP. No . . . that's why I'm asking.
CA. My dear sir, (*with dignity*) a politician . . .
TIP. (*malicously*) You mean yourself?
CA. Excuse me. A politician must–especially in a political crisis such as our country is now passing through, a crisis of a nature to determine a general disturbance, a disturbance which, if we take into consideration the past of any constitutional state, especially a young state like our own . . .
TIP. (*impatiently, tapping his heel*) Please, my dear sir, once more . . . (*incisively*) what do you ask in exchange for this letter? Short! Short! (*repeats Caţavencu's gesture of cutting short*)

CA. Well, if that's how it is . . . if you want it short . . . here you are. I want you (*pleadingly*) not to oppose me; in fact, to support my candidature.
TIP. (*ready to explode*) Your candidature! (*controlling himself*) My dear sir, don't you think you are asking too much?
CA. Then you, who proposed the exchange and are asking me the question, must answer.
TIP. (*drawing up close to Caţavencu; the previous action is repeated*) But, really, don't you think it's too much? Eh? What do you say?
CA. (*innocently*) No.
TIP. (*insinuatingly*) Supposing the Standing Committee were to resign and we reserved a place for our dear Mr. Caţavencu?
CA. (*smiling and genial*) That's nothing, my dear sir.
TIP. Supposing the same Mr. Caţavencu were appointed State Advocate?
CA. (*as before*) That's not much, my dear sir.
TIP. Supposing that Mr. Caţavencu were appointed to the post of mayor, at present vacant, and to that of churchwarden of St. Nicholas'? Eh? (*Caţavencu refuses with a smile*) And supposing the Zăvoi estate on the outskirts of the town . . .
CA. (*smiling as before*) Excuse me, my dear sir. A politician must – he is bound – especially in a crisis such as our country is now passing through, a crisis of a nature to determine a general disturbance, a disturbance (*caressing and mouthing his words and refining his tone and accent*) which, if we take into consideration the past of a constitutional state, especially a young state like our own, which has scarely emerged . . .
TIP. (*tapping his heel impatiently and interrupting him*) Oh! Let's leave the phrases, Mr. Caţavencu. They're all right for mugs. Am I the sort of man you can make drunk on cold water? Tell me what it is to be. Like a man, now; what do you want from me? (*rises, boiling*)
CA. (*rising too*) What do I want? What do I want? You know quite well what I want. I want what is due to me after so long a fight. I want my deserts in this town of nitwits, where I am the first . . . of the political leaders. I want . . .
TIP. (*boiling*) What do you want?
CA. (*similarly*) I want . . . the seat in Parliament; that's what I want! Nothing else! Nothing! Nothing! (*after a pause, with warmth and an increasingly ingratiating tone*) I deserve it. Please don't oppose me. Support me. Adopt me. The day after tomorrow, at the moment when I am returned with the necessary majority . . . at that moment you will have your letter . . . (*with great warmth*) on my honor!
TIP. (*ready to explode*) On your honor! And supposing I can't adopt you?

CA. You can.
TIP. (*losing his temper more and more*) And supposing I refuse? What if I refuse to adopt you?
CA. (*irritably*) You must.
TIP. (*scarcely controlling himself*) You forget that it is not wise to play about with a man like me. No, no, no! I refuse to adopt you.
CA. You must.
TIP. No!
CA. You must, if you care at all for the honor . . .
TIP. (*exploding*) You scoundrel! (*Caţavencu takes a step back*) You shameless cad! I don't know what keeps me from breaking your head. (*rushes, takes a stick from the wall and makes furiously for Caţavencu*) You swine! You must give me that letter here . . . you must tell me where that letter is . . . or I'll kill you like a dog! (*rushes headlong at him. Caţavencu dodges round the table and sofa, overturns the furniture, and rushes to the window, which he flings wide open*)
CA. (*trembling, yells out of the window*) Help! Quick! Murder! The vampire! The thug of a prefect! Help!
(*Zoe enters quickly R.*)
ZOE. (*rushing between Caţavencu and Tipătescu, pleading and very excited*) Mr. Caţavencu, for God's sake, I implore you, stop shouting! . . . Fănică, are you mad? . . . Mr. Caţavencu, I beg you.
CA. (*excited too*) Stop shouting ma'am?
TIP. (*exhausted with emotion, wiping his forehead and dropping on a chair R.*) Swine! Swine! Swine!

Zoe promises Caţavencu that she and her husband will support him. As Tipătescu wearily yields his support as well, Trahanache's voice is heard. They hide, and Trahanache, finding no one, leaves a note for Tipătescu to say that he must see him before the political meeting that evening. When he goes off, the other three come in and are at once joined by the Drunken Citizen, who wants to know how to cast his vote. Tipătescu is urging him to vote for Caţavencu, when Farfuridi, Brînzovenescu, and Trahanache enter and hear him. The ensuing dispute is interrupted by Ghiţă bringing in an urgent telegram from Bucharest; it announces that the government party's candidate in their constituency is to be a stranger–Agamemnon Dandanache.

In Act III the scene is the Town Hall, where Trahanache is presiding at the meeting of electors. Farfuridi is making a speech, which is continually interrupted, and he becomes more and more boring and incoherent. When he finishes, Ghiţă asks Trahanache to suspend the meeting and to come outside for a word with Zoe and Tipătescu. In his absence a quarrel breaks out between the supporters of Caţavencu and Farfuridi, and the hall empties. Trahanache returns, followed by Zoe and Tipătescu, who urge him to nominate Caţavencu. But he triumphantly produces a note of hand with two signatures forged by Caţavencu. The meeting now reassembles. Caţavencu makes a speech, as empty as Farfuridi's, but demagogic in tone and punctuated by applause from his group of supporters.

TR. (*ringing the bell*) Please do not interrupt the speaker, gentlemen!
CA. (*loudly*) I do not fear interruptions, Mr. Chairman. (*to the meeting and especially to his group, in a tone of assurance*) You may interrupt, gentlemen, because I have the courage of my convictions . . . (*returning to the tone of his speech and speaking all the time with unction*) and . . . and . . . of finance! (*prolonged applause*). Yes, we are ultraprogressives, we are free-traders. Now, guided by these ideas, we have founded in our town the "Romanian Economic Dawn," an Encyclopedic-Cooperative Society, independent of that of Bucharest . . . since we are for decentralization. We . . . I . . . do not recognize control over us by the capitalists of Bucharest; for in our own district we can do what they are doing in theirs.
GP. (*applause*) Hear, hear!
CA. Our society has as its aim the encouragement of Romanian industry, because, let me tell you, from the economic point of view we are in a bad way.
GP. (*applause*) Hear, hear!
CA. Romanian industry is admirable, is sublime, one might say, but it is completely nonexistent. What, then, do we and our cooperative acclaim? We acclaim labor and toil, which are unknown in our country!
GP. Hear, hear! (*enthusiastic applause*)
TR. (*ringing the bell*) Gentlemen, don't . . .
CA. Let them interrupt, Mr. Chairman; I'm not afraid of interruptions! . . . In Jassy, for example—allow me this digression; it is sad, but true!—in Jassy we haven't a single Romanian merchant, not one!
GP. (*stirred*) Shame!
CA. And yet all the bankrupts are Jews! Explain that phenomenon, that mystery, if I may so express myself!
GP. Hear, hear! (*applause*)
CA. Well! What does our cooperative say? What do we say? . . . This is what we say; this state of things is intolerable! (*approval from the group. Loudly*) How long are we to have no bankrupts of our own? England has her bankrupts, France has her bankrupts, even Austria has her bankrupts; in short, every nation, every people, every country has its own bankrupts! (*with unction*) We alone have no bankrupts of our

own! (*frantic applause. Pause. The speaker drinks from the glass and again casts flashing glances around the meeting. At that moment several people upstage move, and the Drunken Citizen and Ghiţă in mufti appear, the Drunken Citizen very unsteady. At their entry there is noise*)
TR. (*ringing the bell*) Silence, please!
CA. (*who during the short period of the uproar caused by the entry of Ghiţă and the Drunken Citizen has been consulting his papers; in a dominating voice*) Brothers, this is what the statutes of our cooperative say. Article 1: An Encyclopedic-Cooperative Society with the title of "Romanian Economic Dawn" is formed in our town. The aim of the society is the welfare of Romania and the prosperity of every Romanian.
D.C. (*who from the entrance has advanced unsteadily to C. and collapsed on a chair in front of the rostrum, rises and lifts his hand*) Me too! (*hiccups*) Me too! (*reels and collapses on the chair again. Laughter upstage, uproar down*)
CA. (*to Trahanache, turning toward the chairman's table*) Mr. Chairman, I must ask not to be interrupted.
TR. My dear sir, I thought you said that interruptions . . .
CA. Yes, (*with dignity*) but . . .
TR. Anyway . . . (*ringing*) Don't interrupt, please.
CA. (*feeling for the thread of his speech*) As I was saying, then; "the welfare of Romania and the prosperity of every Romanian. . . ."
D.C. (*rises swaying and lifts his hand*) Me too! (*hiccups loudly; laughter, uproar*)
TR. Shame! (*leaning over the table*) Who are you, my dear sir?
D.C. (*hiccupping*) Mr. Nae knows me (*points at Caţavencu*) . . . "Choclopedic" . . . (*laughter, uproar*)
CA. (*on edge*) What?
D.C. "Romanian" . . . (*laughter; he hiccups*) "Dawn" . . . (*he hiccups; ever increasing laughter and uproar*)

The Drunken Citizen is turned out by Caţavencu's supporters. Trahanache now proposes to announce the name of the candidate. When he utters the name of Dandanache, Caţavencu accuses him of falsifying the nomination. Trahanache retaliates with the charge of forgery. Caţavencu tries to make public the matter of the lost letter; Ghiţă and the government supporters rush to seize him; and the curtain comes down on uproar and scuffling.

Act IV takes place in Trahanache's garden. Zoe is alone with Tipătescu. Tormented because there has been no sign of Caţavencu since the meeting broke up two days before, she fears that he may publish the letter in ignorance of the fact that they hold his forged note of hand. Trahanache comes in with a stranger whom he introduces as Dandanache. The candidate, who is not only chronically muddle-headed but also temporarily bemused by the fatigue of his journey, continually confuses the identity of Trahanache and Tipătescu. Zoe asks Tipătescu whether Caţavencu was not better than Dandanache; he replies that Dandanache is simple, but at least he's honest. When Trahanache has gone off to be present at the start of the voting, Dandanache tells them how he secured the candidature.

DAN. As I was saying, my dear fellow, it wouldn't have done for me not to be elected. I and my family, since '48 . . . fight and fight . . . all the time . . . and to think that I should be left out in the cold just at present . . . without a constituency . . . very nearly not elected, old man.
ZOE. You not be elected with your qualifications! Impossible!
TIP. Impossible!
DAN. My qualifications are all very well, ma'am, but it was a near thing. . . . Ask me, old man, and I'll tell you. The central committee didn't want me and there you are. They said I was not outstanding. Fancy, me not outstanding! I was lucky; very lucky I was. Just listen to this. One evening somebody . . . I won't say who . . . a person of note . . . but a bachelor . . . comes and plays cards at my house . . . and when he goes away he leaves his overcoat behind. Next day, I try to put it on–thinking it's my own–and see that it's not mine. I look through all the pockets and find–what do you suppose?
TIP. What?
DAN. (*laughing*) A letter!
BOTH A letter?
DAN. A love letter?
BOTH (*with emotion*) A love letter?
DAN. A love letter to my bachelor from the wife of a friend . . . I won't say who . . . a person of note. . . .
ZOE. Well?
TIP. Well?
DAN. Well, what do you think, my dear fellow? A cab, lad, quick! I get into the cab and go to the person . . . the bachelor . . . I won't say who . . . a person of note. "Find me a constituency," says I, "or I'll hand the letter to the papers." He argued and argued . . . but he had to give in, ma'am . . . and off goes the telegram here, old man!
ZOE. (*whose agitation has increased as Dandanache's story went on*) Oh. Mr. Dandanache . . . you did wrong! Your action is . . . if you'll excuse my saying so. . . .

TIP. (*quietly*) Zoe! (*Zoe goes upstage*)
DAN. The fact is, my dear fellow, I've changed my politics. What was to be done? If that had hadn't occurred to me, I shouldn't have got a seat. And that wouldn't have done at all, old man. Just fancy! Ever since '48 my family (*coming downstage; to audience*) and I in every Parliament, with every party, as an impartial Romanian should . . . and I to be left without a constituency!
TIP. Exactly. (*biting his lips*) But you haven't told us the end of the story . . . about the letter.
ZOE. Yes, the letter.
DAN. What letter?
TIP. The bachelor's letter.
DAN. What bachelor?
ZOE. (*on edge*) The person of note . . . the love letter . . . your political weapon with which you have got yourself nominated.
DAN. (*at last remembering*) Oh, yes! . . . the letter . . . yes . . . I know.
ZOE. Well, the letter . . . ?
TIP. What happened?
DAN. I have it put away at home . . . you know, in a safe place.
ZOE. Didn't you return it to the person?
DAN. (*in astonishment*) Return it?
TIP. Well, you've been nominated; he kept his word.
ZOE. You ought to give it back.
DAN. My dear madam, why on earth should I give it back? How could I do such a silly thing? I shall need it again another time. In certain eventualities . . . off it goes to the papers! (*comes downstage*)
ZOE. (*disgustedly*) Oh! (*crossing to Tipătescu; quietly and imitating his previous tone of voice*) "He's simple, but at least he's honest!"

Zoe begs Dandanache not to repeat the story at dinner and then takes him off to rest. As soon as she returns to Tipătescu, Ghiţă enters and gets Tipătescu out of the way by saying that he is wanted at the telegraph office. He then tells Zoe that Caţavencu wants to see her. As soon as Caţavencu enters, Zoe proposes that he should hand over the letter in exchange for the forged note. But he reveals that in the fracas at the meeting he lost his hat—and with it the letter. Zoe in desperation shouts for Ghiţă, but instead there appears the Drunken Citizen with Caţavencu's hat. Having once been a post-office sorter, he is scrupulous in handing over the lost letter to its addressee, Zoe. He then asks how he should cast his vote and is told to do so for Dandanache. When he goes off Caţavencu is completely demoralized, but Zoe seizes the chance to win him over and offers to let him off if he will chair the dinner in honor of Dandanache. Caţavencu goes out, dazed but thankful, and she re-enters the house. Trahanache brings in Dandanache, telling him the story of the lost letter. Dandanache then begins his parallel story, but in such a disconnected way that Trahanache cannot follow it. Further disclosures are prevented by Zoe, who returns with Tipătescu and reminds Dandanache of his promise of silence. The stage then begins to fill with people celebrating the election of Dandanache, and the curtain falls on general jollification and reconciliation.

Even so lengthy a summary of the action does not do justice to the ingenuity of the plot, in which the transitions, the exits and entrances are very skilfully contrived. In comparison with *O noapte furtunoasă*, soliloquy is used more discreetly. Though there is not the perpetual motion of a farce, the action is lively and never flags. And the unexpected introduction of Dandanache is a *coup de théâtre*. This inspiration only came to Caragiale while actually writing the play. He is said to have asked his friends' advice as to who should win the election, Farfuridi or Caţavencu? One friend answered "Both!" Sometime later Caragiale said to him: "I have made them both win, as you jokingly suggested . . . but in the person of one man, Agamiţă Dandanache, who is more of a fool than Farfuridi and more of a cad than Caţavencu. That is the dramatic climax, the surprise *dénouement*, which I had been after for two months and couldn't find!"[2]

The striking thing about this comedy is its detachment. Our sympathy is not given to any character or set of characters, nor yet, despite their corruption, are we revolted by any. The prefect Tipătescu is hasty and violent; Zoe is heartless; and both are selfish. The amiable Trahanache is fatuously trusting. Caţavencu is a scoundrel, though his demagogic gifts fascinate us. The policeman Ghiţă is dishonest and unprincipled. Dandanache is not only fatuous but a blackmailer. The Drunken Citizen is a complete sot. And the reconciliation of all these people in the finale is remarkably cynical. Yet as a whole the comedy is delightful and leaves no unpleasant taste behind. The fact is that Charles Lamb's words on Congreve's comedies apply remarkably closely here.[3] "Judged morally every character in these plays . . . is essentially vain and worthless. The great art of Congreve is especially shown in this, that he has entirely excluded from his scenes–some little generosities on the part of Angelica perhaps excepted–not only anything like a faultless character, but any pretensions to goodness or good feelings whatsoever." Substitute Zoe for Angelica, and this last sentence fits *O scrisoare pierdută* admirably. "Whether he did this designedly," continues Lamb, "or instinctively, the effect is as happy, as the design (if design) was bold. I used to wonder at the strange power which his *Way of the World* in particular possesses of interesting you all along in the pursuits of characters, for whom you absolutely care nothing–for you neither hate nor love his personages–and I think it is owing to this very indifference for any, that you endure the whole." That description might have been written of *O scrisoare pierdută*.

CHAPTER 4

Comedies after 1884

BEFORE the first night of *O scrisoare pierdută* Caragiale was already writing his next play. It was to be entered for a competition instituted by the National Theater for plays of at least three acts. The closing date was fixed for January 15, 1885, but later extended to February 15. The title of Caragiale's play was at first *Bărbierul* (The Barber), but finally was *D-ale Carnavalului* (Carnival Doings). On February 15, Caragiale read the play to *Junimea*, and on February 25 the judges announced that it had won the competition.[1] It was produced on April 8, but was withdrawn after its second showing.

The scene is a barber's shop in Bucharest during Carnival time. Pampon enters, looking for Nae Girimea, the barber, but finds only the apprentice Iordache. Pampon produces a season ticket for shaving here, which he has found in the bedroom of his mistress Didina Mazu. Iordache tells him that new tickets have been issued, because with the old ones a certain druggist cheated Nae by using acid to erase the cancellation marks. Pampon jumps to the conclusion that this ticket must have belonged to the druggist. As he leaves the shop, Miţa Baston, in love with Nae, enters and tells Iordache that Nae is deceiving her. When a man with toothache comes for treatment, she slips into an inner room. The man describes himself as a candidate for a post in the Inland Revenue. As soon as Iordache prepares to extract his tooth, the pain goes; this, the candidate explains, is his regular cure for toothache. When he goes out, Miţa re-enters and is left to look after the shop while Iordache goes out to eat. Pampon comes back. He and Miţa soon discover that they are both deceived in love; he tells her how in Didina's room he discovered the ticket and a letter addressed by a woman to "Ducky." Miţa asks for the letter and reveals that she herself wrote it to her lover (meaning Nae). Iordache re-enters warning of the arrival of her protector, Crăcănel. She retires to the inner room. Crăcănel announces that he is prepared to wait a long time for Nae, but Iordache proposes to close the shop. As soon as Crăcănel has left, Pampon asks who he is. Iordache says that he is Miţa's lover. Pampon rushes after him, believing him to be "Ducky."

IORDACHE. That man's a little batty. What sort of customers am I getting today? A fine carnival, this! Let me fetch Miţa out. (*Nae enters*) Mr. Nae, at last! I thought you were never coming.
NAE. Why?
I. Two people have been looking for you.
N. Who?
I. One's name I don't know; the other was Crăcănel.
N. Crăcănel?
I. Yes, and Mrs. Miţa is here.
N. Miţa here? Didn't you tell her that I was not at home and was coming late?
I. Yes, I told her, but she said she'd wait for you till tomorrow or the day after. I took advantage of the opportunity and went to the place on the corner for something to eat. I'd not taken two mouthfuls when in comes Crăcănel and asks the waiter where is Mr. Nae's model hairdressing saloon. I dashed back to warn Mrs. Miţa. The other merchant has been here too; he says that he has a season ticket to change, or something to ask you . . . I don't really know.
N. So Miţa's here?
MIŢA (*who has already opened the door a little and heard Iordache's last words, coming down*) Yes, I'm here, Ducky; are you sorry?
N. (*pretending to be cheerful*) Sorry? Sorry? Of course not.
M. (*crossing to Nae, quietly*) Send Iordache out. I've something to say to you between us two.
N. (*pretending not to hear*) Pardon?
M. Iordache, if you've nothing better to do, be a good boy and leave us; I've something to tell Mr. Nae in private.
I. I'll go . . . and finish my helping of cabbage. (*exit upstage. Miţa goes and locks the door upstage*)
N. Why do you lock the door?
M. (*upstage*) Someone might come and disturb us. I've something to say to you in peace and quiet. (*pause*) Nae! (*she comes slowly down, excited*) Ducky, you don't love me any more (*one step and she stops*)
N. (*hardly turning*) Well now, how did you get that into your head?
M. (*another step*) Why didn't you come the night before last when I wrote to you?
N. (*as before*) I was ill the day before yesterday.
M. (*coming down, energetically*) You're lying! Did you get my note?
N. Yes.

M. Where's my note? Show me my note.
N. (*after looking through all his pockets*) Evidently I've lost it.
M. Lost it? Where did you lose it?
N. How do I know where I lost it? If I'd known I was losing it, of course I shouldn't have lost it.
M. You don't know where you lost it?
N. No.
M. (*sternly*) Ducky! Ducky!
N. Well?
M. You see this bottle? (*takes a little bottle out of her pocket and shows it to him*)
N. Well, what about it?
M. Do you know what it has inside?
N. Ink.
M. Not ink, Nae dear . . . English vitriol!
N. (*stepping back*) Vitriol! Are you mad?
M. Yes, vitriol. Are you afraid?
N. Of course I'm afraid.
M. Why, if you know you are innocent?
N. Because you don't know what vitriol is.
M. Yes, I do . . . a sort of metal.
N. Don't you know what it can do?
M. Yes, Nae dear, it scorches; it burns everything in a moment, Ducky, and especially the eyes.
N. Give me the bottle.
M. Ah!
N. Why do you keep such things? What for?
M. (*ready to explode*) What for? I need it.
N. What do you need it for?
M. (*exploding*) What for? (*with a sweeping gesture, which makes Nae cover his eyes, as he quickly steps back*) For you, Master Nae, and for your Didina!
N. (*turning pale*) What Didina? Do you know what you are saying?
M. You know better than I do. Don't beat about the bush, you humbug. What Didina, eh? Didina, for whom you are betraying me; Didina, whom you love; Didina, with whom you spent last night, you wretch!
N. It's not true, I stayed at home ill.
M. You're lying! Just now you said that you did not know where you lost my note. Let me tell you: my note was found in your Didina's room by her gentleman in question.
N. Gentleman in question? Pampon?
M. You see! you see! you know his name. Yes, a tall, bearded fierce man, with whom you will have to deal this very day, Because he met

me here, showed me my note and I declared to him that the traitor is the same man as is betraying me (*Nae walks about in agititation*), my lover, my faithful lover, to whom I (*broken-heartedly*) have always been faithful.
N. What have you done?
M. Pampon is out to kill you. But before he can have his revenge, I shall kill you myself. I shall kill Didina and you and myself! (*flings herself on a chair in hysterical desperation and hides her head in her hands*)

Nae embraces her, removes the vitriol, and pushes her into the next room as Crăcănel comes in, furious because Pampon has assaulted him. The Candidate returns in the throes of toothache; then Pampon enters and chases Crăcănel out. The curtain falls on the Candidate having the wrong tooth drawn by Nae.

The scene of Act II is a masked ball. Didina is pursued by the Candidate who has been warming himself up with drink. Crăcănel, searching for Pampon among the masks, decides to introduce himself to each man he sees as "Ducky" and to address him as "Iancu" (Pampon's christian name) in the hope of provoking reaction. The Candidate, being thus accosted, thinks that Crăcănel has mistaken him for his brother Iancu; so, for fear of meeting his brother, he rushes off when Crăcănel says that "Iancu" is at the ball. Crăcănel next tries Iordache, who has come in dressed in Nae's costume as a Turk. Miţa, hearing Crăcănel, runs off to change her costume. Nae, the Candidate and Iordache agree to change costumes in order to baffle Miţa and Crăcănel. Crăcănel now makes his approach to a newly arrived mask; as this is Pampon, the reaction is violent. In the ensuing row Crăcănel proves that he is not "Ducky," and it becomes clear to them that someone else is deceiving them both. They discover Miţa in Didina's costume and Iordache in Nae's (as a Cossack). Miţa tells them that "Ducky" is now dressed as a Turk. But when the Turk returns, he is in fact the Candidate. Before he has time to reveal his identity, Miţa throws her bottle of vitriol in his face.

Act III takes place back in the barber's shop. Didina, Nae and Iordache return from the ball and go into the side room when Pampon, Crăcănel, and the Candidate are heard outside. These last break in, looking for "Ducky." They have lit the lamp and entered the side room when Iordache comes in from the street with a subcommissar of police and two sergeants. Crăcănel and Pampon are arrested for shopbreaking and taken away by the sergeants. Before leaving, the subcommissar induces Iordache to take a raffle ticket for a musical tobacco jar. When he has gone, the Candidate appears from the side room, unharmed by the "vitriol" as it was really violet ink. They go out to get him cleaned up, turning out the lamp. Mița and Didina enter separately; Didina relights the lamp. They begin to fight, but Nae comes in and separates them. He takes them off to explain how he has won the gratitude of their protectors by getting them released from the police station. Pampon and Crăcănel now appear with bottles and food, much pleased with Nae. The two women enter and reproach them with deceit in coming to the ball. Nae pacifies everybody, and the curtain comes down on the Candidate having his toothache cured in the usual way.

D-ale Carnavalului had a largely unfavorable reception. It is clear from the press that it was hissed by the majority of the first-night audience, though the gallery enjoyed it and twice called the author on stage after the final curtain. *L'Indépendance Roumaine* described the play as so vulgar and crude that it would delight Zola himself. Caragiale had already suffered from the attitude of most of the adjudicating committee; he knew that they regarded his play as defective from both the literary and the moral point of view. For one thing some of them, particularly Vasile Alecsandri, regarded authorship as an educational vocation and the theater as a school, a view characteristic of their generation of Romanian intellectuals. But the low life of *D-ale Carnavalului*, the brawls of the blackguardly Pampon and the crass Crăcănel and of their mistresses, were presented by Caragiale in a detached way; they were not fitted into a moralizing scheme and made ridiculous for a moral purpose, as Alecsandri would have treated that sort of thing. The affair with the vitriol must have given offense in a different way; the audience is left from the end of Act II to halfway through Act III under the impression that the Candidate has suffered frightful injury. Caragiale's stage direction when he enters in Act III is "*The Candidate's face is covered with patches of black; horrifying entry*." Audiences of the 1970's, accustomed to "kitchen sink" comedy and the Theater of Cruelty would not be startled at the low life or the horror; but to the "high life" audience of the National Theater at Bucharest in the 1880's these things were repulsive. The play was withdrawn after its second performance.

D-ale Carnavalului proved to be Caragiale's last comedy. He turned to other genres, and not till toward the end of his life did he set to work to make a comeback. While living in Berlin, he planned a comedy which would bring back the characters of *O noapte furtunoasă* and some from *O scrisoare pierdută*, a quarter of a century older than when they had last been seen, and much advanced in station. In 1906 he fixed on the title *Titircă, Sotirescu & C-ie* ("Titircă" being Dumitrache and "Sotirescu" Chiriac). There exists a very summary outline of the five acts. But early in 1907 he admitted that it was not going well, and in the autumn that he could not write a line, let alone a scene. Though he seems never to have abandoned the project, nothing came of it.[2] Nevertheless, he did write one more comic piece for the stage, a curtain-raiser called *Incepem*, an occasional piece for the first night (September 12, 1909) of a company organized by Al. Davila. It represents a rehearsal, the start of which is delayed first by the director's secretary, then by a professor of esthetics, then by an aspiring playwright, and finally by an eccentrically dressed lady who declares herself a slave to fashion, but who ends by proclaiming what it is that theatergoers are looking for. This *one-act snapshot*, as the author subtitled it, probably served its purpose adequately, but has not much interest today – though it includes a pleasant pun on "*Tanti Ema*" (Auntie Emma) and "*Tantiema*" (the percentage).

YOUNG MAN: . . . a letter from Auntie.
DIRECTOR: Auntie! Auntie who?
YOUNG MAN: Tanti Ema.
ACTOR: Tantiema! I'll bet you're a playwright.

CHAPTER 5

Drama: Năpasta

THE year 1889 is notable in Caragiale's life and work for more than one reason. It was the year in which he married. It was the year in which he resigned after a brief and unsatisfactory term the only important post that he ever held and one for which he must have seemed beforehand extremely well equipped. It was also the year in which he first turned his hand to serious fiction and drama. The grim story "O făclie de Paşte" was printed in August. The equally grim drama *Năpasta* was finished by December. Caragiale gave readings of it to gatherings of friends; but the fact that it was not read to *Junimea* is evidence that he was already in a less happy relationship with Maiorescu and his group. *Năpasta* seems to have made a good impression at the private readings. Its first public performance took place at the National Theater on February 3, 1890.[1]

The two acts of *Năpasta* are set in an inn in a mountain village. The village schoolmaster Gheorghe is discussing with the innkeeper Dragomir and his wife Anca an item in the newspaper which says that Ion, a forester convicted nine years before of the murder of Anca's first husband, Dumitru, has escaped from the salt mines. Gheorghe suggests that Ion has been shamming madness so as to escape. Dragomir says that at the trial it was clear that Ion was mad. Anca is astonished to hear that Dragomir was present at the trial, and Dragomir is irritated by her interest. She withdraws, but presently returning overhears him ask Gheorge whether it is true that a murderer who confesses his crime after ten years have elapsed, is not punished. When she hears that such is the law, she interrupts.

AN. A fine law, I must say! (*wipes her eyes*)
DR. Why don't you try to make a better one (*glaring at her*) *You* again? (*to Gheorghe*) You see why I didn't tell her . . . every time there's mention of the dead man, or it occurs to her to think of him,

sne howls at me all day. (*to Anca*) Get out of here and don't keep on moaning at me, you misery! (*pause; Anca draws back*) If you intended to spend all your life moaning for your first husband, why did you marry again? Go on . . . get out!

AN. Why aren't you kinder, Dragomir?

DR. Get out . . . at once!

AN. I'm going (*exit up C.*)

DR. Go to the devil! (*rises in anger*)

GH. (*after a pause*) Come, man, you're too rough with the woman.

DR. Now just you leave me alone! Do you know what my life's like? Do you know what I've done for that woman? I'd better have broken my neck before I met her. If that woman weren't so contrary, I'd be a different man today. You don't know what's gone on between her and me.

GH. Yes, yes, I can see what's going on. You torment one another for no reason; you don't suit her nor she you.

DR. She married me so as to have some one to hold anniversaries for the dead man's soul. From the first day of our marriage till now I've never once seen her smile; from that day to this she's lived with her body in this world and her thoughts on Dumitru in the next.

GH. He may have treated her better than you do.

DR. Treated her better! How could she know from the first day that perhaps I might not treat her better than he? Didn't I love her? For if I hadn't loved her . . . ! And anyway, I understand a woman weeping for her husband if she's a widow. But once she's married someone else! Who could put up with that? Why did she marry again?

GH. Hm!

DR. Yes, why? If she can't tear herself away from the dead man's shadow? No, say she's mad and has driven me out of my senses too. Am I in my right mind, do you think, since I married her? Ugh, I've had enough! For eight years on end nothing but Dumitru, Dumitru! I hear him when she's talking; when I look at her, I see him; I live with his ghost in the house, eat at table with it, sleep with it. No, it can't go on much longer! (*Anca comes in quietly up C., stops in the door and listens. Gheorghe sees her and makes a movement. Dragomir, attracted by Gheorghe's movement, turns and sees her*) Look at her! Look at him! It's he, Dumitru! (*to Anca*) Get out! Get out! Quick, don't let me see you! (*Anca stands still, her eyes fastened on him*) Are you going or must I? Don't let me see you! (*starts toward her; she moves toward him; he rushes, seizes her hand, and pulls her firmly downstage*) What do you want? Why do you look at me like that? What are you thinking? Did *I* kill him? Eh? Speak! (*tugs at her*)

AN. (*firmly*) Dragomir, you're mad! (*crosses herself*)

DR. Mad? Speak! (*tugs at her again*)

GH. Dragomir!
AN. Oh . . . mad!
DR. No, tell me. . . . One of two things; either you think I killed him . . .
AN. Really, that's a thing to say!
DR. Yes! If so, why do you go on living with me? Or if you don't think so, then why do you torment me? What have you against me? Let me alone; you and your Dumitru! (*he pushes her with his hand and goes upstage; she tries to take a step toward him*) Let me alone! (*same movements again*) Let me alone! (*he goes out very excited up C., slamming the door*)

Alone with Gheorghe, Anca tells him to let her be; she cannot love him. He replies that he will leave the village. Startled, she changes her tone; in fact, when he goes to the door, she calls him back, tells him that after Dragomir is buried she will be his, and says that, when Dragomir presently comes home drunk and goes to sleep, she will put a lamp in the window as a signal for him to return. Left to herself, she reveals her hatred of Dragomir. Then there is a knock at the door. She opens it to find a stranger, weary and hungry, who begs for food, and says he has fits of madness. Giving him food and drink, she asks how long he has been like this. He says that he has been so since he was a forester at Corbeni ten years ago and was beaten to make him confess to a murder. Anca realizes that the stranger is the convict Ion. She takes him off to lie down. Gheorghe then reappears and tells her that Dragomir, after drinking at another inn, has announced his intention of going away for good on the coming day. Gheorghe is surprised that Anca does not seem pleased. She sends him away to await the signal. She is now convinced that Dragomir is the murderer. Presently he comes home drunk. She taxes him with his intention to leave her, saying that he must be mad to run away and that recently his behavior has been strange, and finally recurs to his suggestion that she believes him to have murdered Dumitru. The act ends with Dragomir going off to bed and Anca saying to herself: "Pray, Dragomir; for the hour is near!"

Act II opens with Anca soliloquizing. No sooner has she made up her mind to murder Dragomir with the ax and throw his body into the well than she hears Ion groaning. She fears that this will waken Dragomir, though she does not wish to kill him in his sleep, since he must know why he is being killed. Before she can enter his room, Dragomir emerges, terrified by a nightmare. She urges him to confess whatever is on his conscience and tries to make him imagine that he sees Dumitru. Suddenly there is a scream from Ion; when he appears, Anca tells Dragomir who he is. She asks Ion about his prison life and his escape. When she suggests that it was not he who killed Dumitru, Dragomir agrees and says that in a year's time Ion will be free. Anca then tells Ion plainly that it was Dragomir who killed Dumitru. Ion in a fury grips him by the throat. But Anca does not wish Dragomir to die that way; she seizes the ax, and Ion, in astonishment, goes out. She runs after him. Dragomir, left alone, bewails his ill luck; he needed only one more year to be safe, but Ion will tell the village. However Ion, who has not left the house, comes in and sits down to eat and drink with Dragomir. He tells him of a fellow convict who was kind to him. This man had allowed his brother to be condemned for the murder of their father, whom he himself had killed. Later he had given himself up, and his brother had been set free. Dragomir, moved, tells Ion that he will take him away and look after him. But Anca has returned without being perceived and overhears; she retires unnoticed. Dragomir fetches money from the cellar; he and Ion are ready to leave. But they find the door locked from the outside; as Dragomir unlocks it, they are confronted by Anca. Ion goes and lies down; Anca tells Dragomir it will be better to keep Ion with them. But Ion has a fit of the horrors. He imagines he is being beaten, and, seizing a knife, he rushes into the next room. Before they can intervene, he returns with the knife covered in blood and collapses; he has stabbed himself. Anca sees her opportunity. The dying Ion asks her to take his money belt to give to his fellow convict. She takes it and puts it in Dragomir's pocket. When Ion is dead, she tells Dragomir that they must throw the body into the well; for if they reveal the death, they will be accused of murder. The now demoralized Dragomir obeys. When they come back into the house, she suddenly asks him if he is not ashamed of murdering Ion.

DR. I . . . Ion?
AN. Yes, Ion.
DR. I . . . killed . . . Ion! (*laughs feverishly*)
AN. You laugh? If not you, who did? (*he looks hard at her; she meets his gaze. She goes to him and takes him by the front of his shirt*) What's this? Is this blood his? Isn't it Ion's blood?
DR. (*quickly fastening his jacket across his chest*) Get away!
AN. Don't button up, Dragomir! There's little on your shirt; but there's plenty in there in the room. Look, here it's covered in blood. Go into the yard; it's sprinkled everywhere. Go and draw a bucket from the

well; you'll find the water red. You murderer, you! You'll rot alive in the damp walls of salt till God thinks the time has come to summon you, so that he may judge you the better.
DR. Judge me for what?
AN. Because you have taken another's life.
DR. Whose?
AN. Ion's.
DR. (*waits a moment and wipes his eyes*) Woman, if someone were to ask you of this, what would you say?
AN. What I have seen.
DR. (*more and more curious*) What's that?
AN. (*simply*) That Dragomir killed Ion, I don't know why.
DR. You would?
AN. (*takes the lamp and puts it at the shutter; then comes downstage*) Although you have been bad to me, I'm still sorry for you, Dragomir. I will give you some advice. If it happens that you haven't the luck to escape in the end . . . if they lay hands on you . . . don't be a fool and don't try to deny it as you do with me, for there you won't be able to play about as you do here; they'll put you to the torture, worst luck. They'll tear your flesh, pull out your teeth and nails . . . break your skull. Listen to me; I'm talking to you for your good. (*she looks impatiently upstage*)
DR. You mean . . .
AN. Do what I tell you. Confess that you've killed Ion, and you'll get off with punishment; you'll escape the tortures.
DR. (*shocked, beating his fist on the table*) But if I didn't kill him?
AN. There we go again! "I didn't." "Yes, you did." "No, I didn't." "Yes, you did."
DR. (*boiling*) Let me alone! (*buries his head in his hands, stopping his ears*)
GH. (*enters quickly, sees Dragomir, and tries to withdraw*) Dragomir!
AN. (*going up to Gheorghe; very swiftly, in a whisper*) Go to the village; get the constable and any men you can find; say that I have sent you about a murder . . . and come with them!
GH. What's the matter?
AN. Go, I tell you . . . you'll see. Come back quickly. (*she drives him out. With a solemn step she approaches Dragomir, who is sitting on his chair with his head in his hands*) Get up, Dragomir; the hour has come!
DR. (*gets up*) The hour!
AN. The hour of reckoning. Stand up . . . gather what wits you still have and answer my questions. . . . Why did you kill him?
DR. (*choking with vexation to the point of tears*) I didn't! *I* didn't kill him. Weren't you here? Didn't you see?

AN. Not Ion. Never mind about Ion. I'm talking about someone else now.
DR. (*turning pale; softly*) Whom?
AN. You know whom; don't pretend! You want to go away; you must go away. (*he nods assent gloomily; she goes on harshly*) Ah! You don't move a step from here till you speak his name. (*looking at him with all her might*) Speak his name once!
DR. (*very softly*) Du . . . mi . . . tru!
AN. (*breathing deep*) You see? Yes, Du-mi-tru! (*sits down; he stands*) Why did you kill him?
DR. For you . . .
AN. For me . . .
DR. So as to marry you.
AN. How did you kill him? Tell me!

When he has told all, Gheorghe and others are heard outside. Aroused and desperate, Dragomir leaps on Anca, but the men burst in and seize him. Anca tells them that the body is in the well and that the money belt is in Dragomir's pocket. Then, when they have bound him, Anca asks for a word alone with her husband, and the curtain falls as she whispers the words: "Retaliation for crime and false witness for false witness!"

Năpasta was not well received. The public fell away after the first night, and the fourth performance was the last. Aristizza Romanescu, who played the part of Anca, described this as the greatest failure of her career. But she added that she was later consoled by seeing that, whoever played the role, the play had the same fate.[2] More serious probably was the attitude of the theatergoers of all classes, who were accustomed to very different fare and had no desire to see a drama of Romanian peasant life, especially one so grim. Nor did most of the critics approve. They largely shared the prejudices of the public. We have seen that C. A. Ionescu was prosecuted in 1901 for writing that *Năpasta* was plagiarized from the work of a Hungarian playwright, who was in fact a figment of his own imagination. Defending counsel had then alleged that *Năpasta* was a plagiarism of Tolstoy's *The Power of Darkness.* Confrontation of the two plays shows that there was no ground for such a charge.[3] Nevertheless, Caragiale had imbibed something of the spirit of Dostoevsky and other Russians; Anca's long-meditated revenge has the monstrous quality of Raskolnikov's insufficiently motivated crime in *Crime and Punishment*, while the conception of the mad Ion suggests something of Tolstoy's imagination.

That the Romanian public was puzzled and embarrassed by the convulsions of Ion—one observer said that she saw the important personages in the audience laughing[4]—is, though understandable, to be regretted; that they did not take the play to their hearts is easy to forgive. In the nineteenth century and the first half of the twentieth, it was normal for a theatergoer to expect to be able to sympathize with at least one of the main characters of a serious play. *Năpasta* is much more a study in abnormal psychology than a tragedy, and as such is more to the taste of the 1970's than to that of 1889. Neither Anca nor Dragomir engage our sympathy. Gheorghe is colorless and a minor figure. It is interesting to see in the half-witted convict Ion, the one type of character for which Caragiale does seem to show sympathy, or perhaps not so much sympathy as an indignant pity for the unfortunate whose weakness of intellect or character gets him pushed around by the harder and more capable members of society. Ion, is, in fact, the tragic counterpart of that comic figure, the Drunken Citizen, in *O scrisoare pierdută.*

To the charge that Anca's psychological processes are improbable, we may answer that precisely their monstrous abnormality interested Caragiale. To the charge of improbability of situation, for example, that Ion should turn up by chance at Anca's door, we may answer that far greater coincidences have been swallowed by critics and public alike, as for instance in the novels of Thomas Hardy. The action is, as a matter of fact, very skilfully developed. The diction and its appropriateness for the peasant characters, a thing difficult for foreigners to judge, was singled out for praise by several critics. To sum up, *Năpasta* deserves greater respect but does not call forth a warm enthusiasm.

CHAPTER 6

Stories in the Mood of Năpasta

I *"O făclie de Paşte"*

AKIN to *Năpasta* in tone are three stories, all with the countryside as their setting. The first of these, "O făclie de Paşte" (An Easter Candle), was published in *Convorbiri literare* for August 1, 1889, and therefore is earlier than *Năpasta*.

Leiba Zibal is the Jewish innkeeper in a Moldavian village where marsh fever is endemic; he and his wife Sura and their boy Strul have all been infected. A timid man, Leiba broods on his fears as he awaits the arrival of the stage coach. He is especially obsessed with the thought of his former employee Gheorghe, a brutal, criminal type who on being discharged had told Leiba to expect him on Easter Eve "so that we can crack red eggs." It is now Easter Eve. As Leiba dozes in the evening sunshine, he has a horrible dream, in which an escaped madman smashes the skulls of Sura and Strul together "like soft eggs." He is awoken, and the stage coach arrives. Two students come in for a drink and describe an appalling crime, in which a neighboring Jewish innkeeper and his family have been atrociously murdered by robbers. As they discuss the theories of Lombroso and other criminologists, Leiba recognizes in their description of the criminal type known as "the case of reversion" the likeness of Gheorghe. As soon as the stage coach has gone, he closes the inn and refuses to open when customers knock.

After his wife and child are in bed, he sits in the entry behind the closed gates. Some riders pass, and he catches a fragment of dialogue which suggests that one may be Gheorghe. Fetching an oil lamp, he sits down again to watch. After the bells have rung for the midnight service of the Resurrection, he hears steps.

A noise of crunching on sand! But he was in his stockings and had not so much as moved his foot. A second crunch. Several more. Obviously there was someone outside, here, very close. Leiba stood up, pressing his hand to his chest and trying to choke back a rebellious lump that rose in his throat. There were several men outside . . . and Gheorghe! Yes, it was he; the hour of the Resurrection had struck on the hill. They were talking softly. "I tell you he's asleep. I saw when he put out the light." "All the better; we'll get the whole brood." "I'll open the gate; I know the knack. Let's make an opening. The beam goes along here." And one could sense the groping movements with which the man outside was measuring the distance on the wood.

A large drill could be heard biting into the dry tissues of the old oak beam. Zibal had to support himself; he leaned on his left palm against the gate and covered his eyes with his right. Then, by an inexplicable whim of his inner workings, he heard with his imagination, very loud and clear: "Leiba! here comes the stage coach." It was unmistakably Sura's voice. A warm ray of hope . . . a moment of joy; it is a dream again! But Leiba quickly withdrew his left hand; the point of the drill, reaching through to his side, had pricked him in the palm. Still thinking of escape? Ridiculous!

In his burning brain the image of the drill took on undreamed-of proportions. The tool, turning on and on, was growing infinitely large, and the hole was becoming bigger and bigger, so big in fact that in its round bore the monster might have appeared standing to his full height. What went on in that brain was passing beyond the sphere of human thought: life had risen to an exalted plane on which everything was seen and felt as enormous, of chaotic size.

. . . The work outside was proceeding methodically and persistently. Leiba had now seen the twisted steel tooth coming out on his side and being withdrawn four successive times. "Now bring the saw!" said Gheorghe. The thin blade of a saw passed through the first hole and began to gnaw away in quick regular movements. The plan was easy to grasp: four holes in four corners of a square: the saw would describe the lines between them. Meanwhile the drill had been fixed in the center of the square; when the piece was wholly detached from the main body of the wood, it would be drawn out; through the space left a strong hand would come in, grip the beam and remove it to one side . . . and the Gentiles would be in Leiba's house.

And the same drill, some minutes later, would be the instrument of torture for Leiba and all his family. Two executioners would hold the victim down splayed out, and Gheorghe, with his heel on the victim's belly, would slowly drive the drill as he had driven it into the beam of dead wood, but this time into the living bone of his chest, deep and still deeper, till it touched his heart, so as to stop its maddened throbs and fix it to the spot!

A deathly sweat bathed Zibal's whole body; the man weakened at the joints and slowly let himself fall to his knees, like an ox which bows its neck beneath the last stroke, knowing that now it must abandon itself. "Yes, fix it to the spot!" thought Leiba, lost. "Yes, fix it to the spot!" And he remained awhile with eyes glaring at the light from the window. For some moments he stood thus, petrified, in another world. But suddenly: "Yes!" he repeated, smiling and blinking savagely: "Yes! Fix it to the spot!"

Then a strange transformation took place in that being, a complete reversal; his trembling ceased, his discomposure vanished, and his face, contorted by so prolonged a crisis, took on a queer serenity. He straightened himself with the confidence of a strong healthy man who is aiming at an object easy to attain. The line between the two upper points of the square was complete. Leiba approached, curious to see the play of the tool. His smile was now still more firmly set. He nodded his head as if to say: "I've still time."

The saw gnawed away the last fibers next to the hole for which it had been making and began to work between the lower holes. "There are three more," thought Leiba, and with the caution of the most experienced of hunters moved quietly into the taproom. He searched under the bar, took something, went back as carefully as he had come, concealing the object which he held in his hand as if he were afraid of the walls being indiscreet, and approached the gate on tiptoe.

But a dreadful thing! The work outside had stopped completely; nothing more could be detected. "What is it? Can they have left? Has he gone?" the thought flashed through the mind of the man inside. And at that supposition he bit his lower lip, filled with an extraordinary depression.

"Aha!" it had been a horrid illusion. The work began afresh, and he set himself to follow it with palpitations of the warmest interest. Undeniably our man was racked with an incomprehensible desire to see the work finished as soon as possible. "Quicker!" thought Leiba impatiently, "Quicker!" Now the bells could be heard again on the hill.

"Quicker, man! Day will overtake us," said a voice outside, as if prompted by the will of the man within. The man with the saw set to work very energetically. A few movements, and all the points of the square were joined. At last! The drill softly withdrew the square section. A big strong hand entered. Before it could touch the beam that it was seeking, two howls were heard, while Zibal firmly tied the free end of his noose round the fixed post by the cellar flap.

The snare was ingeniously contrived: a long rope fastened at one end to a post; at a convenient length a noose which Leiba held open in his left hand, while with his right he gripped the other end tightly. At the required moment Zibal pulled the noose tight and, swiftly gripping the free end in both hands, tugged the whole arm inside. In a flash the operation was complete. It was accompanied by two roars, one of despair, one of triumph; the hand was "fixed to the spot." Then steps were heard swiftly departing. Gheorghe's comrades were leaving Zibal the prey he had so adroitly snared.

The Jew rushed into the taproom, took the lamp, and with a confident twist raised the wick high. The light which had been imprisoned in the bars shot up joyous and triumphant, restoring life and definition to the misty shapes around. Zibal passed with the lamp into the entry. The robber groaned heavily; by the straining of his arm it was clear that he had given up the idea of useless struggling. The hand was swollen and the fingers crooked; it seemed to be trying to grip. The Jew brought the lamp near. A shudder: his fever was coming on again. He moved the lamp too near, so that, as it trembled, it touched the robber's hand with the hot glass. There was a violent contraction of the fingers, followed by a dull moan. At the sight of this phenomenon Zibal started; his eyes flickered with a weird inspiration. He began to laugh with a violence that shook the arch of the entry and went swiftly into the taproom.

Later Sura wakes with the impression that she has heard bellowings. Through the window she sees the approaching candles of the villagers returning from the Resurrection service. When she goes down, she finds Leiba gazing at the shapeless, blackened hand of Gheorghe, fastened above the burning lamp. As the villagers burst in, Leiba calmly rises and walks out, saying: "Leiba Zibal is going to Jassy to tell the rabbi that Leiba Zibal is no longer a Jew. Leiba Zibal is a Gentile, because Leiba Zibal has lit a candle to Christ."

"O făclie de Paşte" shows Caragiale already fully developed as a short story writer. The tale is excellently constructed, with every detail calculated to contribute to the total effect. Clearly it has the same sort of interest as *Năpasta*; the delineation of unusual psychology. The timid Leiba is driven by his terror of Gheorghe's menace, magnified by his whole past experience and distorted by his feverish condition, into committing an act of appalling brutality, quite foreign to his normal ways, an act which appears to leave him demented.

II "*Păcat*"

In 1892 Caragiale reprinted "O făclie de Paşte" in a booklet with "Păcat" (Sin) (which gave the volume its title) and a shorter humorous piece, "Om cu noroc" (Lucky Man). "Păcat" is the longest of his stories in this vein.

Niţă, a country boy training at Bucharest to be a priest, is walking alone in the seminary yard, when a note is thrown to him from a neighboring house. It is a declaration of love. Some nights later, after another such note, he gains access to the lady, the young widow of a boyar, her only child a crazy daughter. After a period of happiness, the affair is discovered by the widow's family. Niţă tries to force his way in, but is badly beaten up. Months later he recovers, though left with a weak heart; but his beloved is now dead and the house is being pulled down.

Ten years have passed, and Niţă, now the priest at Dobreni, is walking in the main street of the county town during the annual fair, when he sees an urchin giving a performance of unseemly song and dance.

A boy of some eight or nine years of age, ragged and dirty with bare feet, clad in unsuitable clothes–a big tail-coat, the waist of which came to his ankles, a battered top hat on his head–was playing the buffoon.

He was a small and very profligate comedian–scraggy, stunted, and pale; his withered calves, visible through the rents in his trousers, were covered with sores. Miserable as he was, he was nevertheless very bold. He was smoking a long cigar, making strange faces, cheeking the boyars and abusing them, calling them by their nicknames. He began to sing a shameful song, playing the castanets, making unforgivable gestures and movements. People were immensely amused. An old peasant woman who was in the front row of the audience, shamed by the refrain which with diabolical intent the boy directed at her, looked for a way to escape the eyes turned upon her, crossed herself and said as she went off:

"What a crime! God protect all children!"

Weary, the little one stopped; he went round greeting the boyars comically with his enormous top hat and sat down on a chair with his legs crossed, next to the senator . . . Another cigar . . . The senator treated him to coffee and rum. A second "friend" encouraged him with another glass . . . and another.

The boy got up and began his dance again. His movements and gestures were now even more profligate. Gradually, however, his limbs lost the sureness and symmetry of their movements; his singing was muffled, his articulation uneven. Another verse! But panting choked him. The singer stopped for a moment, swaying, sagging at the waist; he was yellow as wax; his eyes squinted dully from deep in his head. Then the unanimous prompting of his admirers roused him to a strenuous effort. He sighed deeply, tried to raise his foot, spun round, and his sorely tried body collapsed heavily on the edge of the pavement. Dead drunk!

Profoundly shocked, the priest questions the café proprietor and learns facts from which he realizes that this boy, Mitu, is his own son. His mistress had died in giving birth to the boy. Her daughter had run away too and gone to the bad. Niţă searches the town desperately and, finding the boy asleep in a churchyard, takes him home to Dobreni.

Niţă and his wife Sultana cherish Mitu and set about curing him of his skin troubles and his bad habits. He seems to be dying of consumption, but with the aid of a folk remedy recovers. Meanwhile his whereabouts have been discovered. The procurator comes to investigate and is about to have Mitu removed, when Niţă's brother-in-law intervenes. He shows the priest how to bribe the procurator, and Mitu is left in the care of Niţă and Sultana. But to no one does the priest reveal that he is the boy's father.

In the same year Sultana gives birth to a daughter, Ileana, who grows up wild and passionate.

They once had a calf; they had rescued it from trouble—the cow had died and the poor thing was left without an udder. Who tended it? Ileana—she would then have been a little girl of about twelve. Who fed it? Who had moved heaven and earth to get her mother to let her take the tender calf to bed with her in the house? Ileana. It was an extraordinary affection. One morning, however, she got up sulking; she refused to talk to her mother or father; they, as parents will, seeing her in a bad mood again, reproached her; she ran into the garden. There she tried to play as usual with little Priian; she took hold of him to pet him and, gritting her teeth, gripped him tightly by the muzzle. Either the animal too was in no mood to play that morning, or he found her mark of affection too teasing—he snatched himself away and went off snorting. She called him—he would not come. She followed him—he wouldn't obey. She yelled at him—Priian ran off. And so on and so on. His stubbornness grew in proportion to her insistence. He wouldn't, and that was that. Weary, with all her blood in her cheeks, trembling with rage, she went away, took a piece of maize porridge and a hatchet, and came back again. When he saw her coming, Priian dug in his hoofs and curled his tail. She approached gently, with her left hand outstretched and her right hidden behind her back, speaking caressing words to her friend who had vexed her. He fixed his large, foolish eyes on her, half trusting, half not, breathing at her from the depths of his nostrils the sweet scent of milk. He stood motionless. The girl softly advanced her hand. Priian held out his tender muzzle, but before he could take the morsel, Ileana dealt him a hearty blow in the curly thicket on his forehead; the blade sank deep into the still unformed bone. Priian's pretty head was smothered in blood. The poor wretch rolled over and began to kick desperately.

Her mother saw her coming, gloomy and sprinkled with blood on her cheek, her hands, her chest.

"What's the matter?"

"I've killed Priian at the bottom of the garden. I'll show you!"

When they arrived, Priian was quite dead.

"You wicked girl!" cried her mother. "Why?"

"Just for fun!"

She gave her a sound beating; the girl bore it without a word or a tear. But her mother lamented long, in her sorrow and anxiety.

After Sultana's death Ileana is married to a weak, good-natured husband. She falls in love with Mitu, who is now the village schoolmaster at Dobreni. The priest sees what has happened; he rebukes each in turn. Unable to persuade Mitu to ask for a transfer, he goes to talk things over with his brother-in-law. The latter advises him to let things take their course, but recalls his own youth: how his father had him taken for service in the militia in order to break off an affair which he was having with his brother's wife. The priest decides to go to the prefect of the county, who is the former procurator, and arrange for Mitu to be taken for military service. While waiting his turn for an audience, he sees the prefect's wife in a tantrum, which is followed by a fit, and learns of her mad cruelty to the servants. He is then asked to sit in the drawing room.

The priest passed into the drawing room and stopped a moment in the doorway. It was long since he had entered such a room, since his gaze had encountered such a combination of forms and colors! It was really wonderful. The drawing room gave on to the garden, and the light reflected from the trees, passing through the net curtains, gave still greater charm to that rich and tasteful interior.

The man took a step forward, like a traveler advancing into a valley filled with enchanting memories, which he suddenly sees once more after a long absence. Astonished, he looked around; but when his glance reached the corner where the greenish light from three great windows struck full, the traveler was thunderstruck. A cry was stifled in his breast: his eyes had met the gaze of a large portrait.

It was an apparition from another world—a sweeter, kinder, happy world! It smiled with the same unforgettable smile, in which great gentleness mingled with great passion, such clear intelligence with such blind impulse. The old man stood a long, long while in front of her and, as if wanting to kindle with his gaze the motionless eyes above him and make them blink just once, he nodded his head and whispered:

"Well! you should know what is in my heart now!"

"I beg your pardon, father?" said the prefect.

The old man started:

"Who is it?" he asked, stretching his hand toward the portrait on the wall, without looking at the man who was rousing him so abruptly from his reverie.

"My mother-in-law . . . the mother of my wife. An unfortunate woman; she died young, poor thing!"

The old man turned mechanically.

"Well, now! What is it? Tell me your trouble," added the prefect. "Please sit down."

The priest sat down and was silent.

"Have you some dispute . . . some affair?" he went on.

The priest said nothing.

"We are alone, don't be shy. No one can hear us. Speak out," said the prefect, very benevolently, but with something of impatience. "I'll do anything possible for you, knowing you as I do."

The old man slid from the chair and crumpled on the soft carpet. The constable, who was waiting outside for orders, was fortunately ready at his superior's call to help the invalid; he loosened his neck, his chest, his belt, and rubbed his temples and his heart with vinegar. When the priest came to, he was lying on the sofa in the office. He quickly did himself up, made his excuses—he was ill, palpitations and dizziness—he had felt himself going, everything turning dark around him, sleepiness. He got up, said good-bye and made to leave.

"Well, but you've told me nothing," said the prefect, signing to the constable to go away.

The constable went out, very pleased with the humanitarian service he had performed. The priest kept on searching in his breast, at his belt, in his pockets, without saying a word. The prefect said wearily:

"Come on! tell me once and for all."

"I've lost it," the priest answered naïvely, took his leave and went out quickly.

Niţă returns home, and going to Mitu, reveals that he is his father and Ileana his half-sister. Appalled, Mitu leaves the village. But on the third night he returns to see Ileana once more and is overcome by her passionate longing for him. As the first light appears, the priest goes to open his window and sees them in a parting embrace at the door of her house. He takes his gun and shoots them both dead. Then he rings the church bells. As a crowd gathers, he leads them to the corpses. He bends to unclasp the arms of Ileana from the knees of her half-brother, with the words "Not like that, you bitch. It's a sin!" Then, as he rises, his heart disease strikes him down.

If *Năpasta* could be criticised for straining the probabilities, "Păcat" is still more open to the charge. That the child whom Niţă is moved to rescue should not only be his own son, but should be revealed as such by facts in the possession of the café owner, and that the prefect should have married the daughter of Niţă's mistress, strains the probability more than the plot of *Năpasta.* Caragiale here treats a theme akin to that of *Wuthering Heights*, introducing coincidences and cruel tricks of fate characteristic of the novels of Thomas Hardy, but does not add the powerful ingredient of landscape as Emily Brontë and Hardy do. Objections of improbability might not even occur to us if the structure of "Păcat" were as satisfying as that of Caragiale's most masterly stories. There is not here that perfect organization of detail to achieve a total impression.

III *"În vreme de război"*

Caragiale's other story in this vein, "În vreme de război" (In Time of War), was printed in 1898. It opens at the time of the Russo-Turkish War of 1877 with the capture of a band of robbers, who have been operating for two years, breaking into houses and even murdering. Iancu, the priest at Podeni, had been found tied up, after a raid on his house. On the evening after their capture, Iancu, who had been away, returns home and hastens to see his brother, the innkeeper Stavrache. When they are alone, Iancu confesses that he has been the robbers' chief, though he tried to stop the murder. The raid on his house had been a blind. He had only escaped capture with the rest by a chance. While the two men are talking, a band of volunteers on their way to the front call at the inn. After carousing they lie down to sleep. Stavrache suddenly has an inspiration, which he communicates to his brother. Accordingly, the priest's hair is cut close, his beard shaved, and he goes with the volunteers to enlist.

Presently a letter comes from Iancu, saying that he is about to take part in the attack on Plevna in Bulgaria. It is shortly followed by another letter, in a strange hand, announcing his death. As their mother had died in the meantime, Stavrache is left in sole possession of the property. Five years pass. Stavrache begins to be haunted by ghostly visitations from his brother, once as an escaped convict, another time as an army captain. Each time Iancu says, "Did you think I was dead, brother?" Then one night in a blizzard two men on a sleigh ask for shelter. Stavrache lets them in and goes to fetch food for them. When he returns, the one to whom he has spoken is still standing, while the other is lying down with his face to the wall and has begun to snore.

"Let him rest: he's very weary," said the one standing, and sitting down alone at the table, he began to sup with great heartiness. As he ate, talk naturally began:

"Tremendous blizzard, sir!"

"But where are you from?"

"Far away."

"And where are you going?"

"I don't know. Believe me, I don't know. My friend has brought me along just for company, and see what vile weather we're caught in!"

"Strange what you say," said the innkeeper, raising his eyebrows, "a man traveling around like that without knowing where he's going."

"Ah, well, you see," replied the guest simply.

And he went on calmly with his supper. After reflecting a little, the host continued.

"You are . . . merchants?"

"No."

"Officials?"

"Not exactly officials, you know; but . . . something of the sort."

"I understand: you're making an inspection, as they say."

"No, we're not."

After a pause, during which the guest drank two glasses of wine one after the other:

"Bravo! It's good wine you have, Mr. Stavrache."

"How do you know my name is Stavrache?"

"My friend told me."

"But he . . . how does he know?

"How can I tell? He told me on our way, as I was afraid we should be out all night in this weather; 'Don't worry,' says he, 'we'll put up near here at Stavrache's inn.' "

"Evidently he must know me," said the innkeeper, and started to approach the bed for a better look at the man who was sleeping with his face to the wall. When suddenly:

"How can I help knowing you, Stavrache, if we're brothers by birth?" said the man on the bed, laughing and rising to his feet in front of the innkeeper.

Iancu explains that the letter announcing his death had been a joke. Now he is in desperate need of money and has come to Stavrache for it, asking for it not as a matter of right, but of kindness. Stavrache lies down on the bed and begins to snore and groan like a man in a nightmare. Then, when Iancu touches him, he stands up foaming at the mouth and attacks him. At last the two friends overpower him and tie him up. When the candle, extinguished in the struggle, is relit, Stavrache begins to sing like a priest. As the two men gaze at him in horror, Iancu says "I have no luck!"

The natural interpretation of the story is that Stavrache, being obsessed with retaining possession of his brother's property, imagines his brother's return to oust him, and that, when in fact Iancu does return, without resentment and asking for money not as a right but as a kindness, it is Stavrache's obsessive guilt that makes him violent and brings on his seizure. The text, however, explicitly states that the first "visitation" by Iancu takes place five years or more after the war. Yet at the final confrontation Iancu says to Stavrache (according to the original printed text): "I've not troubled you for two years." We are therefore left in doubt; were the earlier visitations ghostly or real? If ghostly, how does the real Iancu know about them? This difficulty must have occurred to Caragiale's son Luca when he reprinted this tale in the volume *Reminiscenţe* (Reminiscences) after his father's death, because he altered the phrase "for two years [*de doi ani*]" to "for so long a time [*de atîta vreme*]."

Paul Zarifopol praises this least well-known of Caragiale's stories in this genre, especially noting an episode (omitted from the above synopsis) in which a small girl comes to buy some paraffin and some plum brandy just before the arrival of the two men and is caught by Stavrache in the act of stealing a pretzel, an episode which Zarifopol feels gives the haunted Stavrache "most artistically a moment's rest among these slight irritations which bring him back to his healthy commercial interests."[1] However this may be, "În vreme de război" is the least memorable of Caragiale's "sensational" stories, and its omission from the volume *Momente* (Moments), which he published in 1901, suggests that the author did not wish to reprint it.

CHAPTER 7

Stories and Sketches, 1890–1901

THE decade following Caragiale's dramatic period is characterized by the writing of sketches and stories, mainly humorous and with a contemporary setting, though in "Hanul lui Mînjoală" (Mînjoală's Inn) he anticipated the successes in more fanciful writing which marked his subsequent years in Germany.

The jokes and little sketches which he had contributed to the magazines *Ghimpele* and *Claponul* in the 1870's are now of little interest. The only interest, for instance, of the following item is that it contains the phrase "gap [*lacună*] in the law," which over twenty years later was to be the theme of the amusing sketch "Lacună."

How unfortunate are both the lack of foresight among legislators and the gaps in the laws, can be illustrated by the following mishap to a lady of Tîrgovişte.

The lady started a petition for divorce in the appropriate court, on the ground that her husband refused to take her to Bucharest to see the Tsar.

The judge regretfully pointed out to the lady that unfortunately for her, the legislator had here, as in many other places, allowed a gap to find its way into the civil code–since, among the grounds for divorce, he had forgotten to include "the husband's refusal to take his wife to see the Tsar."

If there is no promise of the mature Caragiale to be discerned in this, it must be remembered that it was with such snippets that even Anton Chekhov made his debut in Russian comic papers about the same time.[1]

In the subsequent decade, when Caragiale's creative powers had been primarily devoted to writing plays, he had from time to time produced pieces of prose which do retain interest. Thus, the anecdotes from his youthful experiences in the prompter's box, "Din carnetul unui vechi sufleor" (From the Notebook of a Former Prompter), printed in *Convorbiri literare* in 1881, give an amusing picture of Romanian stage life around 1870. It was in the 1890's that he turned from the mood of "O făclie de Paşte" to produce humorous sketches and stories, which he polished with a care that few other such contributions to the Romanian periodicals of the time were receiving.

I "*Vizită*"

Some of these are concerned with domestic life. "Vizită" (Visit) shows the narrator paying a call on an overindulgent mother, bringing a large rubber ball as a present for her only child, Ionel, on his eighth birthday. The boy, dressed as a cavalry major, makes a nuisance of himself, blowing his trumpet and beating his drum, and dashes with drawn sword at the maid when she brings in the coffee tray. His mother, intervening, receives a blow from the sword on her cheek. When peace is restored, the narrator takes some jam and begins to sip his coffee.

"You don't mind tobacco smoke?" I asked Madam Popescu.
"Of course not! We smoke in this house; my husband smokes and . . . this gentleman . . . I think he rather likes it too."
As she said "this gentleman," his mother laughed and pointed to the major.
"Ah, yes," I said, "this gentleman too."
"Yes, yes, you should see how funny he is with a cigarette in his mouth, you'd die of laughing . . . just like a grownup."
"Oh, that's not good, major," I said. "Tobacco's poison."
"Then why do *you* smoke?" interrupted the major, working away with the spoon in the jam pot.

Ionel goes out and returns with the pot empty. Taking a cigarette from the narrator's case, he smokes it to the end. Then he begins to bounce the ball.

"Ionel! Be quiet, darling! You'll break something. Do you want to annoy me? Do you want mummy to die?"
But the major had a grudge against the ball, which had slipped out of his hand; he bounced it angrily on the floor. I was putting my cup to my mouth, but, as the French say, *entre la coupe et les lèvres* . . . the ball knocked the cup from my hand, scalding me with the coffee, which poured over my best duck-egg trousers.

"Look what you've done! Didn't I tell you to be quiet? See, you've annoyed the gentleman. Another time he won't bring you any toys!"

Then turning to me, with great good humor:

"It's nothing, it'll come out. Coffee doesn't stain. It comes out with a little warm water."

But before she could finish, I suddenly saw her face transfigured with a profound terror. Then she uttered a scream and rose from her chair;

"Ionel, darling, what's the matter?"

I turned and saw the major, white as chalk, with his eyes turned up and his dear little face contorted. His mother rushed toward him, but before she had taken one step, the major fell flat.

"Oh dear!" screamed his mother. "My child's ill! Help! my child is dying!"

I lifted the major and swiftly loosened his tunic at the throat and chest.

"It's nothing!" I said. "Cold water!"

I sprinkled him liberally, while his distracted mother tore her hair.

"You see, major?" I asked him, after he began to revive, "you see? Didn't I tell you that tobacco's not a good thing? Another time don't smoke!"

I left Madam Popescu reassured with her dear major out of danger, and went out. I put on my snowshoes and my overcoat and left. When I got home, I realized why the major had gone out for a moment into the hall with the jam pot–to pour jam into my snowshoes.

"D-1 Goe" (Mr. Goe) is another spoiled child who makes himself a nuisance on a railway journey. "Bubico" is an equally spoiled lapdog, which provokes the narrator into dropping it out of the window of the railway carriage. The conversation of Bubico's mistress and her sentimental fussing over her pet define her clearly as quite a different personality with a different social background from either Madam Popescu in "Vizită" or the mother and grandmother of D-1 Goe.

"Nice little dog you have," I said to the lady after a few moments of silence, "but fierce!"

"Oh, he's not fierce," said the lady, "not when he's used to people. You've no idea how good and faithful and clever he is! He's like a human being; only he doesn't speak."

Then, addressing the basket very affectionately:

"Where's Bubico? Bubico's not there!"

A sentimental whine was heard from the basket.

"Shall the little boy's mummy give him some sugar? Bubico! Bubi!"

The little boy poked his head and ribbons out. His mummy unwrapped him from the rugs in which he was stewing and took him out. Bubico looked at me, uttering a muted growl. Seized with panic at the idea that the wretched creature might try to challenge me, I said to the lady:

"Madam, for God's sake, stop him from jumping at me! I'm nervy, and I don't know what I might do . . . out of terror."

But the lady, taking her pet in her arms and caressing him very tenderly, replied:

"Oh dear! What are you thinking of? We're a good boy and well brought up. We aren't vulgar like Bismarck."

"What?" said I.

"Miss Papadopol's officer's Bismarck."

With this explanation the lady extracted a lump of sugar from her handbag:

"Who likes sugar?"

Bubico (*begging nicely on the seat, despite the swaying of the coach*): "Wuff!"

"Shall mummy give her boy some sugar?"

Bubico: "Wuff! Wuff!"

And he took the piece of sugar and began to crunch it. From another bag the lady produced a bottle of milk, some of which she poured into a glass—then:

"Who likes milky-wilky?"

Bubico (*licking his muzzle*): "Wuff!"

"Shall mummy give her boy milky-wilky?"

Bubico (*impatiently*): "Wuff! Wuff!"

"Phew!" I thought to myself with a deep sigh, "I hope the stray dogs' man gets you, Bubico!"

But the lady tilted the glass to her pet's muzzle, and he proceeded to lap and lap and lap, until a passenger appeared at the door of our compartment and looked in. Bubico stopped lapping and started barking wildly, with bulging eyes, snapping and grinding his teeth and coughing and . . .

"You mangy little brute!" thought I to myself, and all sorts of ideas began to pass through my mind, each more cruel and infamous than the last.

The passenger had withdrawn from the window. Bubico had calmed down. The lady again poured some milk into the glass and drank it herself. I felt black thoughts filling me, increasingly irresistible.

"By the way, madam," I said, "you were speaking just now of Bismarck, who belonged to . . ."

"Miss Papadopol's officer."

"Oh! What is Bismarck?"

"A yard dog. He nearly killed Bubico. Miss Papadopol has a little bitch, Zambilica, a very pretty little thing. She lives next door to me; we're friends. And he (*pointing to Bubico*) makes love to her! (*to Bubico*) Flirt! (*to me*) The wretched maid, a perfect fool . . . I told her when she took him outside in the morning–you've no idea how clean he is!–'Take care he doesn't get away,' I said, 'Or he'll go off to Miss Papadopol's again, and Bismarck will kill him' . . . that's the dog belonging to the officer who is her tenant (*coughs meaningly*). . . . I was doing something in the house when I heard howls and screams outside. 'Bubico!' I cried, 'Bubico! Where's my boy?' I rushed out. There was the fool bringing him to me in her arms; she and Miss Papadopol and the officer's batman had only just got him out of the big dog's mouth. What do you think? Stretched out unconscious and limp as a rag. 'Oh dear!' I said, 'my boy's dying!' I sprinkled him with water and put eau de cologne to his nose. I'm the only one that knows what I suffered. Two weeks he lay there. I even got the vet in. But in the end, God be praised, he came round. (*to Bubico*) Is my boy going to Zambilica's again?"

Bubico: "Wuff!"

"For Bismarck to eat you, you flirt!"

"Wuff! Wuff!"

II *"O lacună"*

In "O lacună" (A Gap) two clerks, Lache and Mache, leave their office in the evening. Mache is to dine with Lache, his wife, and sister-in-law. Lache is in no hurry, but Mache, who is engaged to the sister-in-law, is anxious not to keep the ladies waiting. In a bar Lache becomes involved in an argument over the death penalty, the absence of which, he maintains, is "a gap" in Romanian law.

"But when it comes to a case like this, I mean, so that one ceases to feel that one's life is safe in one's own country . . ."

"Bill!" shouts Mache, banging on the table.

". . . when any assassin paid by a criminal hand can come, I mean, under the pretext of politics, and in your own country, when you are living peacefully and your conscience is satisfied that you have done your duty thoroughly, and you are entirely innocent . . . can come, I mean . . ."

"Bill! Bill!" shouts Mache, banging hard on the table.

"But wait, old boy!"

"It's late, Lache."

"Late?"

"It doesn't do to keep . . ."

"Wait a moment! . . . Can come, I mean . . ."
"Bill!"
"Oh! . . . No, excuse me, we must have the death penalty!"

So it goes on. This extract exemplifies Caragiale's method of relying very largely on dialogue and of establishing his characters' identity by their repetition of certain "tics." For example, "It's late, Lache." His technique as a comic playwright is continued in many of his sketches.

III *"Petiţiune"*

Of this a very good example is "Petiţiune" (An Application), in which a clerk in an office is bothered by a man with a hangover, who comes to find out about an answer to an application, but is so muzzy that the clerk has to cross-examine him to find out what he wants.

"I gave in an application. I want to know what has happened to it. Give me a number."
"Didn't they give you a number when you handed in the application?"
"No."
"Why didn't you ask for one?"
"*I* didn't hand it in."
"Who did then?"
"I sent it by someone else."
"When? What day?"
"About two months ago."
"Don't you know when?"
"How should I know?"
"What do you mean? What's your name?"
"Nae Ionescu."
"What did you apply for?"
"I didn't apply for anything."
"What!"
"It wasn't my application."
"Whose was it then?"
"A friend's."
"What friend?"
"Ghiţă Vasilescu."
"What was he applying for?"
"Nothing."
"What do you mean, nothing?"
"Nothing; it wasn't his application."
"Whose was it then?"

"An aunt of his. He knew that I was coming to Bucharest and gave it to me to bring."

"What's the name of Mr. Ghiţă's aunt?"

"I don't know."

"And you don't know what she was applying for?"

"Yes, I think that she was applying for . . ."

"What?"

"A pension."

The clerk, losing his temper and shouting:

"Look here, this is the Monopolies Office! We don't take applications for pensions here. Go to the Pensions Office; that's where they take applications for pensions."

"Really? In other words, the Pensions Office?"

An even more complete absence of narrative is found in "Telegrame," which consists entirely of a series of telegrams, in which an incident among the local politicians of a provincial town becomes ridiculously exaggerated, all ending happily in a reconciliation, rather in the mood of *O scrisoare pierdută*.

If the background of Caragiale's employment at the Tobacco Monopoly is reflected in "Petiţiune," his experience of schools and teachers as an inspector is reflected in several sketches including "Lanţul slăbiciunilor" (Series of Soft Spots). In this the narrator is asked by a woman friend to get a schoolmaster to give one of his pupils a better mark, so that he does not miss promotion. The narrator loses her letter, finds she does not know the boy's name, goes to the woman who asked her help, finds *she* does not know, and so on. Each person in the chain has been asked because someone else has a "soft spot" for that person and will help pull strings.

IV "*Ultima oră*"

Caragiale's experience of journalism is reflected in many sketches, perhaps most brilliantly in "Ultima oră" (Stop Press), in which he makes fun of a reporter's readiness, during a crisis between Romania and Bulgaria, to seize on the most dubious piece of information and blow it up. The reporter has told the narrator about a Bulgarian terrorist being arrested and locked up in a nearby Chasseurs' barracks. While the reporter is on the telephone, the narrator talks to a Chasseurs officer and finds that there has been no such arrest.

When the captain had taken a few steps, back came my reporter from the telephone, frowning hard.

"You don't know . . ."

"Yes, I do," I said. "I know that your Bulgarian at the Chasseurs' barracks doesn't exist. I've just been speaking to the captain"—and I pointed to the captain, who was moving away through the crowd. "He told me that it's all nonsense; that nothing's ever been heard of any Bulgarian at their barracks."

"Oh, really? . . . The fact is there's no Bulgarian at their barracks . . . *now*. Why? Because they didn't look after him properly and let him get away. It's a good job I discovered that! But anyway that's not so important; it's stale. Let me tell you what I've just heard on the telephone from Bucharest. It's very bad. War has been declared."

"What!" I said, appalled.

"Twenty-three Romanian officers and thirteen soldiers engaged in exercises on the banks of the Danube, between Călăraşi and Giurgiu, have been surrounded by the crew of a Bulgarian gunboat, which had landed on our soil. They were disarmed, made prisoner, loaded on to the gunboat, and taken across to the Bulgarian bank."

"Really?"

"So you see we can't stand by with folded arms. Wait a moment. I'm off to the telephone to give details of the Bulgarian's escape."

"What Bulgarian?"

"The Bulgarian who escaped from the Chasseurs' barracks."

"What details, man? How do you know the details?"

"What's that to you?"

And with that my friend rushed to the telephone.

I got up, stifled with the news of war. I needed to move about; I couldn't stay still.

A few steps away was a group of gentlemen, including a minister whom I had the honor to be acquainted with.

I approached him with due respect and greeted him. The minister answered very politely and held out his hand. I was very surprised that the minister did not seem particularly excited at the Bulgarian gunboat's coup.

"Excuse me, sir," I ventured. "Is it true?"

"What?" asked the minister, smiling as if he knew what emotions were racking me.

"A Bulgarian . . ."

"Gunboat . . . !" said the minister, broadening his smile.

"Yes," I said.

"Don't worry! They haven't taken any Romanian prisoners yet."

Then, to everybody:

"Really, these men will drive people out of their senses."

Then, to me:

"Well, how do *you* come to believe such nonsense?"

"Well, sir, how can I tell what to believe and what not to believe? For example, the story of the Bulgarian's escape."

"What Bulgarian?"

"The one who was caught last night at Valea-Largă and shut up in the Chasseurs' barracks on the hill. They say he succeeded in escaping."

The minister and the rest of the group began to laugh.

"And the anarchist," I went on, "that they let escape at Buşteni on his way from America with four kilos of dynamite."

"Didn't I tell you," said the minister, "that they'll drive people out of their senses? Just see what a state they've brought this gentleman to . . . a man of letters too!"

With these words the minister said good-bye, and after putting fresh heart into me by assuring me that war had not broken out and was not going to break out, he moved off.

When the reporter returns, the narrator feeds to him sensational items which he implies that he has learned from the minister.

"O zi solemnă" (A Solemn Day) is concerned with the earnest Leonida Condeescu, mayor of Mizil, who is bent on raising the dignity of that obscure country town. When an express train from Bucharest to Berlin via Breslau is put on, Leonida, after much hard work, secures a triumph; the express will stop for one minute at Mizil. But this is not enough; he is off to Bucharest to ask that the direction board shall read "Bucharest-Berlin via Mizil-Breslau."

V *"Două loturi," "Cănuţă om sucit," and "Inspecţiune"*

All the sketches mentioned above are lighthearted. But there are from this period stories with more serious undertones. "Două loturi" (Two Lottery Prizes) is on the surface a ridiculous tale of a clerk named Lefter Popescu who has shares in two tickets in two different lotteries. When his partner, Captain Pandele, comes and tells him that in both lotteries they have won first prize, he is unable to find the tickets. He sends a note to his boss at the ministry, asking for leave on grounds of sickness, and for three days he and his wife turn the house upside down, searching for the tickets. At last, exhausted, they take a rest.

Mr. Popescu must have dozed for about a quarter of an hour, when suddenly he jumped up, his face lit with the rays of truth. "I know where they are . . . I know now. Ah! I've found them!"

"Where?"

"In my gray summer coat. I was wearing it in the pub when I bought them. I remember now, I put them in the inside breast pocket. They are there for sure! Bring me the coat!"

The more clearly Mr. Popescu remembered, the more disturbed Mrs. Popescu became. She turned red and yellow.

"Which coat?" she asked in a daze, as though from another world.

"The gray one."

"Lefter!" she cried, putting her hand on her left breast as though she had felt a cruel stab.

"What?"

"I've given it away."

"What have you given away?"

"The coat."

"Which coat?"

"The gray one."

"Who to?"

"Didn't you say you wouldn't wear it again?"

"Who to? Who did you give it to, you idiot?"

"To an old-clothes woman."

"What for?"

"For some plates."

"When?"

"The day before yesterday."

"The day before yesterday! Without looking through the pockets!"

"I did look," she replied, appalled at her crime, "there was nothing in them."

"Shut up!" shouted Mr. Popescu brutally. "How many plates did you get for it?"

"Ten. I bargained for quite a time; she refused to give me a whole dozen," she replied, without knowing what she was saying.

"Where are the plates? I want to see the plates. Bring the plates!" ordered Mr. Popescu sternly.

His wife obeyed without a word. She brought them and put them on the table. Pretty plates with a double border, a broad crimson one inside, and another narrow pink one round the rim. Mr. Popescu took one and rang it–porcelain!

"Splendid! You have good taste!" he said with a sardonic grin. And, smash!, he hurled one to the ground . . . to smithereens, and crash!, another followed.

"Lefter!"

"I'm like this. Open-handed! When I feel like it, I break and break. Plates at ten thousand francs a time, when I feel like it! I break them, damn it, I break them!" And on he went, smash! crash! to the very last one, while his wife shuddered at each breakage as if he were lashing her with a whip of fire.

When he had finished the lot, Mr. Popescu pulled out his handkerchief, wiped the sweat from his forehead, and sat down gravely on his chair; then, in the stern but calm tone of the inflexible judge to the criminal who stands before him:

"What old-clothes woman? Do you know her?"

"Tzica, the young pretty one who always comes here," answered the guilty party, weeping heartbroken with belated regret.

"Do you know where this woman lives?"

"She says that she lives right on the outskirts, in the Farfurigii district."

"That'll do, you idiot!"

Popescu and Pandele accompany the police commissar of the Farfurigii district, Turtureanu, in a cab to the home of the Gipsy Tzica. They knock on the door of the hovel, and it is opened by a ragged girl.

In the living room, which was lit by the flickering of some embers on the hearth, there was a strong smell of meat cooked with plums. An old Gipsy woman was preparing supper. All the visitors retreated to the verandah, holding their hands to their noses.

"Where's your ma, girl?" asked the commissar.

"She'll be coming any moment now," said the child, looking nervously at the three gentlemen.

"Light a candle and take us into the bedroom to wait for her."

The girl hesitated.

"Come on!" roared Mr. Turtureanu, and all three entered, pushing the girl in front of them.

"What's the matter?" asked the old woman, getting up from the hearth where she was huddled.

"We have business with your daughter Tzica."

"Something is missing from a house; *she* knows what's missing," added Mr. Popescu.

"Dear me, sir!" said the old woman, "that's not like Tzica. All the big houses know Tzica. All the great ladies know Tzica."

"Come on, stop chattering and light the candle!" ordered Captain Pandele. "How long do you mean to keep us standing?"

"I'm lighting it now. But it can't be Tzica, sir. God forbid! I could put my hand in the fire for Tzica. Perhaps some other old-clothes woman."

And with these words the old woman lit a tallow candle and passed into the bedroom, followed by the gentlemen. The room contained two beds, a table, a settle, a chair, and an iron stove. On both beds were piles of old clothing, footwear, hats, shawls, and under the beds and on the settle a stock of china and glass of all sorts.

At the sight of the mounds of old clothes Mr. Popescu trembled. He rushed forward and began to rummage through them, taking each article separately and examining it thread by thread. How many reflections, ironical, piquant, sentimental, could be passed on such a motley heap of old clothes, with reference to the vanity of the passing world through which they too passed for a moment, new and unfaded! But Mr. Popescu had no time to philosophize. He searched and searched. Calamity! The gray jacket was nowhere to be found. While thought after thought was streaming through his head, in came Tzica, scarcely able to carry her basket full of old clothes, very tired from a whole day's running about, and hungry too. From a distance her nostrils expanded in answer to the call of the generous smell from the hearth.

As she entered, all three guests surrounded her. Mr. Popescu seized her by the bosom of her dress.

"Where's my coat?"

"What coat?"

"The gray coat."

"What gray coat?"

"The coat with the tickets."

"What tickets, sir?"

"You're pretending you don't know, Gipsy!"

"God strike me if I do!"

"Better speak out," said Mr. Turtureanu.

"If you tell us, you'll get a good tip," added Captain Pandele.

"What is she to tell, sir?" said the old woman frantically. "What's she to tell? Good gracious, if she doesn't know. . . . Just listen to them! What's she to tell?"

Tzica is subjected to a bullying examination. As she is pregnant, she is wearing the jacket under her dress to keep her warm. When she strips it off, the tickets are not to be found. The three women are taken to the police station for further examination but are later released by a visiting inspector with apologies, without anything having been discovered. Popescu, still convinced that they have the tickets, goes at daybreak to their hovel to persuade them to go shares, but is attacked by them and rolled in the mud. When he gets home, he finds a note from a colleague, saying that the boss will sack him if he does not return to work at once.

At five past eight Mr. Popescu, washed and changed, climbed the steps of the Ministry. He asked the porter:

"Has the chief arrived?"

"This very minute," was the reply. "He left orders that you were to go to him immediately."

Mr. Popescu hurried on and went in very humbly. The chief, who was walking up and down with his hands in his pockets, stopped when he saw him.

"So you've come in?"

"Yes, Mr. Georgescu."

"I'm not Mr. Georgescu here, man! Here you call me 'Sir.' Bring the Goldstein file at once. And another time, understand, I'll sack you. The State doesn't pay its employees to drink all night and lie in bed all day—just look what a wreck you are!—instead of coming to work. Do you hear me? Go and fetch me the file!"

The employee stumbled out. He went to his desk, opened the drawer, and grabbed irritably at a wad of papers. As he was putting them on the desk, a little paper, folded in two, slipped through his fingers on to the floor. He bent down, picked it up, stared at it—and gave a yell. All the gods, all, are dead, all die! Only Luck lives and will live alongside of Time, both of them immortal! They were here, here, the tickets; here was the shining sun so long blindly groped for in the dark!

Mr. Popescu was calm—that calm of the sea, which, motionless at last, wishes to rest after the turmoil of a raging hurricane; its surface is smooth and unruffled, while in its depths lie so many wrecks of ships, swallowed up for ever before they could reach harbor. In his breast, between his vest and his skin, in a linen envelope, lay hid the two little pieces of paper with crimson print, like the border of some plates for ever perished. Smiling at this visual memory, he buttoned his waistcoat leisurely, sat down on his oilcloth chair, and with a firm hand indited on a sheet of official notepaper the following composition, which beneath its laconic form concealed so much irony:

"Sir,

My delicate state of health no longer permits me to endure the various vicissitudes of the service.

I therefore respectfully request you to accept my resignation from the post which I hold in this Ministry.

I remain etc.

Eleutheriu Poppescu"

He then took the file and his resignation and went firmly in to the chief, who was working with his nose buried in his papers.

"Sir, here is the Goldstein file."

"All right," answered his superior without raising his head. "Leave it here."

"And also, Mr. Georgescu, if you please, here's my resignation."

"All right. Leave it here."

"Good morning."

"All right. Go away."

Ten minutes later the man who had finally shaken off the yoke of intolerable servitude, entered the bank where the tickets had been deposited *en gros.*

"Excuse me, where does one cash the prizes in the lotteries which were drawn the day before yesterday?"

"The fund is deposited at the safe deposit, but they can be cashed through us as well. Have you a winning ticket?"

"I have two winning tickets," answered Mr. Popescu unaffectedly and showed the tickets from a distance, holding them gracefully between two fingers.

"Are they big prizes?"

"Fairly big . . . I have both first prizes."

The banker opened his eyes in admiration and said, offering to take the tickets:

"Allow me, please."

But Mr. Popescu quietly withdrew his hand, unfolded the tickets and asked:

"Haven't you the official lists?"

"Yes. Here they are."

"Now," said Mr. Popescu sharply, "we have first: nought-seven-six-three eight-four Constantza University."

"No," replied the banker, "one-nought-nine-five-two-nought."

"Don't muddle me, please; one-nought-nine-five-two-nought Bucharest Astronomical."

"No, excuse me," said the banker, "Bucharest Astronomical nought-seven-six-three-eight-four."

For no reason that he could understand, Mr. Popescu felt faint and sank, white as china, onto a chair beside the counter, mechanically holding out his hand with the tickets. The banker took them, looked carefully at the lists, at the tickets, and at their owner, and smiling unaffectedly, said to Mr. Popescu, who was listening dazed:

"See how it is, my dear sir. You've made a mistake . . . and this is why. You have . . . an odd thing, I must say! . . . How can it have happened? Quite extraordinary! You have in one lottery precisely the ticket which has won in the other, and . . ."

"And what?"

"And vice-versa."

When he heard the word "vice-versa," Mr. Popescu turned livid and jumped up, bursting out with tremendous volubility:

"Vice-versa! Impossible, man! Quite impossible! Vice-versa! That's eyewash, see! I'll teach you to play these infamous tricks, to make a mock of people! It's exploitation; you're as insatiable as vampires. Every honest man loses the sweat of his brow because he trusts blindly in your humbug. All this dirty Jewish jobbery on the exchange! We are fools, we never learn sense and come and rebel. Rebel, see! Yes, fools! fools! fools!"

And he began to bawl and slap himself over the eyes and beat his hands with his fists and stamp his feet and make such an uproar that the banker had to ask help of the police to get rid of Mr. Popescu.

The story, as can be seen, is not mere lighthearted fun, yet it is not heavily moralistic either. There is serious social criticism, criticism of the behavior of the police; there is the theme of the man persecuted by ill luck, which is found so frequently in Caragiale's work. But the ending is lighthearted, an epilogue which delightfully mocks sentimental fiction.

If I were one of those self-respecting and respected authors, I should finish my tale thus:

"Many years had passed. Anyone who then visited the convent of Tziganeshti might have seen there an old nun, dark, tall, and withered like a saint, with a large hairy mole over her left eyebrow and with an ecstatic look. She never uttered a word and refused to answer any question. She did no harm; in fact, she was very gentle. One habit alone betrayed that beneath her calm forehead a disordered mind flickered. All day long Sister Elefteria collected from wherever she could find them, bits of plates which she hid carefully in her little low-roofed cell.

At the same time, far off in Bucharest, passers-by might have seen a little old man, washed out and wrinkled, strolling calmly, with that calm of the sea which, assuaged at last, wishes to rest after the turmoil of a raging hurricane. The little old man had his regular stroll—in the morning, up and down in front of the University—in the evening, when the stars were rising, round the Fire Service Observatory at the fork of Bulevardul Pake—whispering all the time in a gentle voice the same word: 'Vice-versa . . . yes, vice-versa!' A word vague as the vagueness of the vast sea, which, beneath its unruffled surface conceals in its mysterious rocky depths innumerable ships, shattered before they could reach harbor, lost for ever!"

But . . . as I am not one of those authors, I prefer to tell you frankly: after the row at the bank I don't know what happened to my hero and Mrs. Popescu.

"Cănuţă om sucit" (Canutza, an Awkward Customer) is a piece of blackish comedy. Cănuţă has a hard life, partly from the cruelty of fate, partly from his own perversity. "Being a Romanian, he took part in politics. He always abandoned the opposition, on the ground of its unbounded and unjustified violence, on the very eve of its coming to power, and always joined the government, which after all was not so much to blame, a few days before it passed into opposition." Finally, he dies after a trifling vexation–not being able to borrow a small sum of money from a friend who had helped him in the past with bigger loans.

Seven years later, they performed the usual ritual of digging up his bones and washing them. His wife and several relatives were present at the service. When the gravediggers struck his coffin and gently raised the rotten lid, lo and behold, instead of Cănuţă's bones being straight out and his face upward, his skull was nape uppermost and his shanks were drawn up toward his rib-case.

"This man was not properly dead when they buried him," said the priest.

"Oh!" replied the woman, "I should have been surprised to find him lying properly. Your Reverence never knew the late Cănuţă . . . an awkward customer."

"Inspecţiune" (Inspection) has the same background of clerks and minor officials relaxing in Bucharest bars and cafés as so many other sketches by Caragiale. As a group is discussing the case of a cashier who has decamped with most of the money in his care, Anghelache, reputed a model of honesty and correctness, fires up and proclaims that the man was the victim of other people's negligence, because his accounts had not been audited for years. The uncharacteristic violence with which Anghelache maintains his view astonishes his friends.

"How long do you suppose it is," cries Mr. Anghelache, "since any one came along and checked my accounts?"

"How long is it?"

"Ten years, ever since I took over . . . the curs!"

"Because they all know that you are a reliable official."

"Reliable!" shouts Mr. Anghelache, boiling, "Reliable! How do they know that I am reliable? . . . The swine!"

And he lifts his glass to his mouth.

"Who can suppose that you are not an honest man?"

Honest! . . . When he heard that word, Mr. Anghelache stood up straight with his glass held high and in a paroxysm of rage:

"I won't have you making stupid jokes at my expense, you idiots! I'll break your heads!"

He flings the glass on the marble table, shattering it to splinters, and goes out of the door in a rage. Every one in the bar gazes at the tables, where his friends are left speechless. For some minutes, while the waiter is clearing up the traces of Mr. Anghelache's fit of violence, they all keep silent, each seeking an explanation in the eyes of the others.

"I've got it!" says one.

"I tell you, he's been up to something!" adds another.

"He's done for, poor chap!"

They are joined by an inspector, who mentions that he is going to examine Anghelache's accounts in the morning. The friends, now convinced that Anghelache has been peculating, are desperate to find him and warn him of the inspection. After searching in vain all night, they give up. When the inspector makes his visit, he cannot inspect the cash because the safe is locked and Anghelache cannot be found. Then the evening papers announce that Anghelache has been found hanged and his body taken to the morgue. Next day the inspector has the safe opened and finds everything in perfect order. The three friends go to the Morgue.

They approached the table on which their comrade lay.

"Why, Anghelache? Why?" asked the youngest, weeping like a fool.

But Anghelache sensibly refused to answer.

Caragiale used to say: "Why should Anghelache have killed himself? Even I don't know that."[2] Nevertheless it is a satisfying story.

VI *"O reparaţie"*

Caragiale is very sparing in the description of nature, only using it where it is necessary for his story, and never for its own sake, never for a "purple patch." As his purpose is usually comic, it is not very often necessary. But when he does use it, it is all the more effective. Thus there is a sketch called "O reparaţie" (An Act of Redress), an anecdote of a hermitage where three old monks and a dumb half-witted gipsy suffer by a bear stealing the fruit from a fine apple tree. The opening paragraph sets the scene:

Lost in the midst of wooded hills, on a knoll sloping down steeply on all sides, stands the little monastery of Schitul-Mărului; a chapel in the middle and four cells surrounding it. The court is enclosed by a fence. Down in the gully to the south is a spring–such cold sweet water is found only at Schitul-Mărului. The main entrance is also on this side–a solid stile barring the path up from the spring. In the middle of the court, in front of the chapel, rises an apple tree of unknown age, which bears princely apples of extraordinary size and flavor.

The Gipsy has tried to chase the bear away, but it has knocked him down. Next day he lies in wait for it by the stile; with one blow from his staff he breaks the bear's head as it appears, but himself falls back with bloody foam on his nose and mouth. The same blow has caused the death of both man and beast.

We raised the dead man and took him into the cell, where Father Ieronim presently lighted a candle at his head, saying: "God forgive the madman! It is good that he has rid us of the beast!" But it was the hour of vespers. Father Ieronim seized the rope of lime bark and began to toll the bell, looking affectionately at the old apple tree. No hero ever had so many voices of bronze to tell the world of his worthy end as our dumb Gipsy!

Schitul-Mărului has only one bell, and that not a big one . . . but it is enough. When the clear sound of the bronze set off on its way to break the boundless silence of that wild solitude, hundreds of other voices came to life one after another on all the hills to vie in answering it, and when the last sound died away in the court of the monastery, and the tongue of the bell ceased to swing, echoes could still be heard dying away little by little, one after the other, in the distant depths of the forest.

VI "*Hanul lui Mînjoală*" and "*La conac*"

The background of nature and of a country inn is essential to "Hanul lui Mînjoală" (Mînjoală's Inn), the finest work of this period in Caragiale's life. The narrative is worked out with such subtlety and irony that a précis of the plot can give little idea of its fascination. The narrator is on his way to his future father-in-law, Colonel Iordache, for his betrothal ceremony. The tale opens with a soliloquy.

A quarter of an hour to Mînjoală's inn . . . from there one stage to Upper Popeşti . . . an hour and a half at a moderate amble. He's a good horse. If I give him corn at the inn and rest him for three quarters of an hour, that'll do. In other words, one quarter plus three quarters, one hour; with an hour and a half to Popeşti, makes two and a half. It's past seven now; by ten at the latest I shall be at Colonel Iordache's. I'm rather late: I ought to have left earlier, but anyway . . . they'll wait for me all right.

He has often called at the inn in the past. The landlady, Marghioala, the widow of Mînjoală, has done wonders in improving the inn; people have even suspected her of dabbling in magic. When he reaches the inn, he hands over his horse to an ostler and goes into the taproom.

"Where's the mistress?" I asked the boy at the bar.

"At the oven."

"It must be warmer for her there," said I, and passed through a passage from the taproom into the kitchen.

Very clean in the kitchen . . . and steamy, not as in the taproom with damp furs, boots and shoes, but with hot bread. Mînjoală's widow was watching the oven.

"Well found, Mrs. Marghioala!"

"Welcome, Mr. Fănică!"

"Would there be anything to eat?"

"Yes, even at midnight—for a gentleman like you."

And Marghioala quickly told an old hag to lay the table, and then went up to the fireplace and said:

"Look, take your choice."

Marghioala was handsome, strapping, and bright-eyed, I knew. But never since I had known her—and I had known her a long time, so often from a child had I called at Mînjoală's Inn in my late father's time, for this was our way to town—never, I repeat, had she seemed more delightful. I was young, good-looking, and impudent—more impudent than good-looking. I went up to her on the left side and, as she bent over the hearth, I put my arm around her waist; when my hand reached her right arm, hard as rock, the devil tempted me to pinch her.

"Haven't you anything better to do?" said the woman, looking at me haughtily. But I, to placate her, said: "Wonderful eyes you have, Marghioala!"

"But suppose your father-in-law hears you?"

"What father-in-law? How do you know?"

"You think that, if you hide under your hat, nobody sees what you are doing. Aren't you on your way to Colonel Iordache's to be betrothed to his eldest daughter? . . . Now, then, don't look at me like that; go into the other room and have your supper!"

I have seen many clean restful rooms in my time, but never one like that. What a bed! What curtains! What walls! What a ceiling! All white as milk. And the lampshade and all, crocheted in all sorts of colors . . . and as warm as underneath a broody hen's wing . . . and a smell of apples and quinces.

I went to sit down at the table and, according to the habit I had learned in childhood, I turned to see which way was east, so that I could say grace. I looked carefully right round all the walls–not a single icon. Marghioala asked me: "What are you looking for?" "The icons," I answered. "Where do you keep them?" "To hell with the icons!" said she. "They only breed worms and bugs."

There was cleanliness for you! I sat down at table crossing myself according to custom, when suddenly there was a yell. I had trodden, evidently with the heel of my boot, on an old tomcat which was under the table. Marghioala darted quickly and opened the door; the angry cat dashed out, and the cold air burst in and put out the lamp. She fumbled for the matches; I searched one way, she searched another–and we met breast to breast in the dark. With my impudence I took her firmly in my arms and began to kiss her. She was half unwilling, half complaisant; her cheeks were burning, her mouth cool, and the peach-down had bristled up beside her ears. . . . Finally in comes the maid with a tray of food and a candle. Presumably we have been looking for the matches for a long time; for the chimney of the lamp was quite cold. We lit it again.

When coffee comes, he finds he has stayed not a mere half hour but two hours and a half. Though a storm has blown up, he is determined to leave. So he goes out, saddles his horse, and returns to say good-bye to his hostess.

She was sitting, lost in thought, with my hat in her hand, and kept on turning and twisting it.

"How much to pay?" I asked.

"You'll pay me when you come back," replied my hostess, looking deep into the bottom of the hat. And then she rose to her feet and handed it to me. I took my hat and put it on my head, a bit on one side. Looking her straight in the eyes, which were glittering very oddly, I said: "I kiss your eyes, Marghioala."

"Good luck to you!"

I flung myself into the saddle; the old maidservant opened the gate, and out I went. Leaning with my left palm on the horse's flank, I turned my head. Over the high fence I could see the door of the room wide open, and in the doorway the white shape of the woman shading the curve of her brows with her hand. I kept on at a slow walk, whistling a love song as though to myself, till as I turned the corner of the fence on to the road, the picture in the door frame disappeared from view.

"Gee up!" I said and crossed myself; then I clearly heard the door bang and a cat howl. My hostess knew that I could no longer see her and had hurried back into the warmth and, of course, had caught the cat in the door. That damned cat was always getting between people's legs.

As the storm rises, he feels a burning pain in his head and takes off his hat. The horse too is stumbling and exhausted; suddenly it stops dead at the sight of a small creature leaping about.

It was a very nice black kid which quietly allowed me to pick it up. I put it in the right-hand saddle bag on top of some clothes. Meanwhile, the horse was shuddering and trembling in all his limbs as though in a deadly fever. I mounted; he started off in a daze.

For a long time now he went like a stone from a sling, jumping over holes, over molehills, over logs, without my being able to stop him, without my recognizing the surroundings or knowing where he was taking me. During this gallop, liable at any moment to break my neck, with my body frozen and my head on fire, I thought of the good shelter which I had foolishly abandoned. Why? Marghioala would have given me her room; otherwise she would not have suggested my staying. The kid moved in the bag to settle itself more comfortably. I turned my gaze on it. Quietly, with its intelligent head thrust out of the bag, it too was watching me. I remembered other eyes. What a fool I had been! The horse stumbled. I stopped him by main force. He wanted to start off again, but fell exhausted on his knees.

Suddenly the moon, appearing through a break in the clouds, shows him that he has lost his way.

I crossed myself, as I peevishly squeezed the horse with my numbed calves to make him rise—then I felt a violent convulsion by my right leg. A scream! I had crushed the kid! I quickly put my hand in the saddle bag; it was empty—I had lost the kid on the way! The horse got up, shaking his head as though he were dizzy. He rose on two legs, flung himself on one side and hurled me off on the other; then he dashed off across country as though nipped by a gadfly, and vanished in the darkness.

Picking himself up, the narrator learns from a peasant that he is near Mînjoală's Inn.

In a few steps I reached the gate. In Marghioala's room there was a light, and shadows were moving on the curtain. Some other wiser traveler must have come in for that clean bed. I was left to put up with a bench by the oven. But by good fortune, when I knocked they heard me. The old maid-servant hurried to open to me. As I made to enter, I tripped on the threshold over something soft . . . the kid . . . the very same one . . . it was my hostess's kid! It too entered the room and went to lie down quietly under the bed.

What was I to say? Had the woman known that I was coming back? Or had she got up early? The bed had not been slept in. "Marghioala!" That was all that I could say, and wishing to thank God for saving my life, I tried to raise my hand to my forehead. Marghioala quickly snatched my hand and, pulling it down, took me with all her strength into her arms.

He is rescued from Marghioala's clutches by his father-in-law, runs away from him three times back to the inn, and is only cured by forty days of penitential fasting in a monastery. Years later as he is chatting to his father-in-law, the new is brought of Marghioala's death.

Mînjoală's Inn had been burned to the ground, burying poor Marghioala, now decrepit, under a gigantic mound of embers.

"So they put the silly woman on the fire in the end!" said my father-in-law with a laugh. And he made me tell him the above story for the umpteenth time. The Colonel stuck to it all along that the lady had put spells in the crown of my hat and that the kid and the cat were one and the same . . .

"Hm!" said I.

"It was the devil, believe me!"

"Maybe," I replied, "but if so, Colonel, the devil evidently gives one a good time . . ."

"He gives you a good time at first, so that you'll get a taste for it, and then—the devil knows what sort of time he'll give you."

"But how do you know?"

"Never you mind!" answered the old man, "that's another story!"

"Hanul lui Mînjoală" was published in *Gazeta săteanului* (The Villager's Gazette) in 1898. Two years later there appeared in the same journal a much shorter story by Caragiale called "La conac" (At the Inn), which has affinities with it. A young man is riding to town to pay the rent of his father's strip of land. As he approaches an inn, he is overtaken by a trader. Riding on together, they pass a church. The young man crosses himself, whereupon he hears a laugh and turning round, finds that his companion has vanished. Then he sees him outside the inn. Once inside, the trader plies the youth with drink and incites him to make love to the girl who serves them. After she has left the youth, the trader induces him to join in a game of cards with some barley merchants. Among them, however, happens to be the lad's uncle, who warns him not to play, but without effect. By three in the morning the lad has lost everything. The players go to bed. Then the trader offers the youth a handkerchief steeped in an anesthetic and tells him to put it to the noses of the sleepers. Sighing, the lad crosses himself, and, as before, his companion vanishes—this time, not to return. Next morning the uncle asks his nephew how much he has lost, gives him the amount of the rent from his winnings, and boxes his ears. Later, when the youth is returning from town, he passes the inn again and sees the girl looking at him, but urges his horse on their homeward way.

The two stories have in common not only the motif of the young man stopping on his journey at a country inn and succumbing to the fascinations of a woman, but also certain details of expression: in each opening paragraph, when the traveler on his "ambler" (a horse trained to move both legs on the same side simultaneously) calculates the timing of his journey; then later, when the traveler, turning on his horse to look back at the woman, finds that he has gone round a corner, so that the inn is no longer visible.

In comparison with "Hanul lui Mînjoală," "La conac" seems commonplace. In the former, the supernatural element is very subtly handled; there is always a natural explanation provided to satisfy the rationalist, and it is supplied with the tongue in the cheek. It is hard to believe that Caragiale wrote the cruder tale after the masterly one. More probably "La conac" is an earlier attempt, laid aside but later published to keep the pot boiling. Yet it is to be noted that not only did Caragiale publish the two stories in the same journal, but he also reprinted both in the volume *Momente.*

CHAPTER 8

Stories and Sketches after 1901

AFTER his removal to Germany, Caragiale was no longer dependent on journalism for a living; he had private means and could write when and what he chose. A few sketches of the old sort appeared, at longer intervals, such as "Duminica Tomii" (Low Sunday), in which Caracudi, the reporter who was hero of an earlier skit on journalism, "Reportaj" (Feature Article), makes a fresh appearance; and "Repaosul Duminical" (The Sabbath Rest), a typical description of a "pub crawl." But in the main Caragiale devoted himself to two types of story; one in a folk-lore vein, the other with an Oriental flavor.

I "Mamă . . ." "Calul Dracului," and "Poveste"

There are three stories in a folklore style: "Mamă . . ." (Mother), "Calul Dracului" (The Devil's Horse) and the unfinished "Poveste" (Tale).

In "Mamă" . . . , an emperor, as he goes away to war, tells his childless wife that he expects to find a baby when he returns. In despair she adopts a Gipsy baby, taking its mother as nurse. When the child grows up, his "parents" arrange a marriage with a king's daughter. The irony of the tale is that it is the "nurse" who insists that he shall not lower himself by marrying anything less than an emperor's daughter.

"Calul Dracului" tells of an old beggar woman who takes pity on a young wayfarer. By the roadside in the moonlight she gives him food and drink; then, as she is telling him a story, he falls asleep.

The old woman leaned over on one side to see whether he was properly wrapped up, for she was sorry for him. When she looked closely, she saw that the boy's covering was rather raised on one side. She pressed it down . . . the blanket rose up again; again she smoothed it down . . . up it came. The old woman said to herself: "Let's have a proper look" and quietly drew back the blanket, put in her hand, and came upon a tail! . . . "I see!" She gently replaced the blanket on the sleeping boy and began tenderly to stroke his hair; she started from the nape and when her hand approached his forehead, she came on two hard bumps—there was no doubt about it—two regular little horns.

She wakes him and asks him to come for a walk. He says he will only ride and suggests that she take him on her back. Eventually she agrees. As soon as he puts his arms round her neck, she changes into a splendid young girl like a goddess and is off with him like the wind. She had been under a curse as a punishment for witchcraft; only if she succeeds in deceiving the devil, can she return to her real identity as a princess (and that only at night). As the first light shows, the ride ends. She returns to her roadside fountain as a beggar again.

"Poveste" was clearly going to be a nouvelle; even in its incomplete state it runs to something like seven thousand words. Like "*Mamă . . .*" it uses the style and names of a folklore tale, but has no magical element. The theme is the ambitions and intrigues of Floarea, the daughter of the Lily Emperor, after her marriage with the son of the Peony Emperor. At the point where the tale breaks off, her sons have married and a grandson is born. From the project which exists among Caragiale's papers it seems that after poisoning her daughter-in-law, Floarea was to be executed by her grandson. These three tales in the folklore vein give pleasure by their language, which Caragiale writes convincingly. But in "Poveste," the theme, which is treated without irony, seems at variance with the fairy-tale setting and language; in the end, it is unsatisfactory. Perhaps the matter of "Poveste" would have been better suited to the manner of "Păcat."

II *"Pastramă trufanda"*

Far more successful was Caragiale's employment of the Oriental style. In April, 1909, he had published "Pastramă Trufanda" (Prime Pastrami) with the subtitle "Oriental Anecdote." When later he reprinted it in the volume *Schiţe nouă* (New Sketches) he added a note to the effect that he had heard it in childhood from a Bulgarian barber in Ploieşti, had later found a variant of it in a French version of the Turkish anecdotes of Nasr-Eddin-Hodja, and, as it was not included in Anton Pann's Romanian version of that collection, he wrote it as best he could remember in the form given to it by the barber. A Turkish merchant, Yussuf, is going on business to Jerusalem. Just as his ship is about to sail from Cavalla, a Jewish neighbor, Aron, hastens on board and asks him to take a sack to his brother Shumen in Jerusalem. The sack, he says, contains old clothes left by his father.

In the evening the traveler found his friend's sack useful; he made a pillow of it and, the sea being calm, he slept peacefully until daybreak; but all night he dreamed that he was eating something salty—naturally, as he was breathing the sea air.

When he awoke, he felt very hungry, and again he thought that he could smell pastrami. He drank a cup of coffee; he smoked a pipe; his hunger seemed to be assuaged; and he lay down again with his head on the sack. After staying like that for a little, he got up again:

"Well!" he said to himself, "I've been to sea before; but such a pleasant smell of pastrami . . . what can it be?"

As he bent down to collect his carpet and pillow, he felt the smell still stronger. He put his nose near the sack and knew for sure that, whatever it was, it was coming from the sack. He untied the string and undid the sack; lo and behold what did he find? The sack did not contain clothes; it was crammed full with prime pastrami.

"Damn that humbug Aron! In case I should be tempted to taste a morsel of his pastrami, he told me it was clothes!"

And as he thought about it, his mouth began to water. He took his knife from his belt, a piece of bread from his pack, and a hunk of meat from the sack. He cut a slice and tasted. A marvelous fragrance! Yussuf made a good meal and tied the sack up again.

By the time the ship reaches Jaffa, all the pastrami is gone, so at Jerusalem Yussuf does not bother to give the empty sack to Shumen. Returning to Cavalla, he tells Aron what he has done and undertakes to pay. Aron begins to howl and beat his head and bang it on the ground; then he drags Yussuf before the Cadi for judgment.

"Well," said the Cadi, "if the man doesn't deny it and undertakes to pay honestly to the last farthing, why do you go on making a fuss, eh?"

"Pay?" howled the Jew, "Pay? Pay for what? For father? Can he pay for father?"

"What father?" asked Yussuf.

"My father."

"What father?" asked the Cadi.

"My father, Leiba Grosu, who is dead . . . and Yussuf has eaten him."

"Whom have I eaten?"

"Father!"

"When did I eat your father, man?"

"When he was on the ship."

"Was your father with me on the ship?"

"Yes."

"And I ate him?"

"Yes."

"Effendi Cadi," said Yussuf, "don't you see that the Jew is mad?"

"I'm not mad!" shrieked Aron. "*You* were mad, to eat father!"

"Tell me again: what father?"

"My father, Leiba Grosu, who is dead . . . haven't I told you?"

"There, Effendi!" said Yussuf.

"Stop shrieking, curse you!" shouted the Cadi. "Stop it! I don't understand a thing. Don't you say your father is dead?"

"Yes."

"Well, if he's dead, how could he go by ship?"

"But he did."

"After he was dead?"

"Yes."

"How?"

"When father died, he made me swear to send him to be buried in holy ground at Jerusalem; that was where he wanted to molder away. I thought to myself that bones don't molder; I buried them here and made the flesh into pastrami."

Yussuf suddenly turned yellow and seized his stomach.

"And," continued Aron mournfully, "I thought, why not save money on the transport? I put the pastrami in a sack and gave it to Yussuf to take to Jerusalem. . . ."

The Cadi, after hard thought, decides to make the Turk pay the Jew for pastrami at the current price and the Jew pay the Turk for deceiving him. "And then with a short Turkish word he turned them both out."

III "*Abu-Hasan*"

"Abu-Hasan" was first published posthumously in a volume with that title in 1915. It is a translation from the *Arabian Nights*, being a shortened version of the story called "Le dormeur éveillé" (The Sleeper Awakened) in A. Galland's French text.[1]

To summarize very briefly, Abu-Hassan habitually entertains one guest each night, a foreigner whom he picks up at the bridge of Baghdad. One evening he chooses a man dressed as a merchant, who is in fact the Caliph Haroun-al-Rashid in disguise. The Caliph slips a powder into Abu-Hasan's wine, has him carried to the palace, and arranges that when he awakes, he shall be treated as Caliph. At the end of his day as Caliph Abu is again drugged and taken home. Awaking, he cannot believe that he is not Caliph and treats his mother roughly. He is removed to a madhouse, from which he is not released until he agrees that he has been mad. He resumes his old habit of inviting one guest.

One evening the Caliph appears again in his disguise and persuades the reluctant Abu to receive him once more. The opiate is again administered and Abu taken to the palace. This time the Caliph bursts out laughing as he watches Abu from his hiding place and reveals himself. Abu is compensated for his sufferings by being allowed to live in the palace and marry a dancing girl.

At this point Caragiale leaves Abu-Hasan living at court happily married. His treatment of Galland's text throws a light on his own methods as a storyteller. In the first place, his version is about half the length of Galland's. The leisurely and repetitive story of the French version, very suitable in the context of the whole *Arabian Nights' Entertainment*, where Scheherazade's object is to spin out her tale, becomes in Caragiale's version much more incisive. Secondly, the rather formal literary language used by the speakers in the French version becomes in the Romanian far more racy. It has the flavor of the language spoken at a period when Romanian society was less westernized than at the beginning of the twentieth century, and thus the language fits the atmosphere of the tale.

This is a convenient context in which to mention other translations by Caragiale. Of most general interest are four tales by Edgar Allan Poe, translated from the French version of Baudelaire. Caragiale's versions of "A Tale of Jerusalem" and "The System of Dr. Tarr and Prof. Fether" were printed in 1878, those of "The Masque of the Red Death" and "The Cask of Amontillado" in 1898. Here the shortenings are slight. It is not surprising that the author of "O făclie de Paşte" should have been interested in tales by the author of "The Pit and the Pendulum." One other story by an American author was translated by Caragiale: Mark Twain's "The Notorious Jumping Frog of Calaveras County," printed in 1894 as "Broasca minunată" (The Marvelous Frog).

CHAPTER 9

Nouvelle: Kir Ianulea

KIR IANULEA, published in 1909,[1] is here placed last as being the masterpiece of Caragiale's last period, the years in Germany. In 1910, when it was reprinted in the volume *Schiţe nouă*, he added a note to the effect that the story appeared under the title "Novella di Belfagorx" in Giovanni Brevio, Rime, Rome, 1545; that in 1549 it appeared under the name of Machiavelli; and that La Fontaine put it as "Belphégor" in his collection of *Contes*, Paris, 1682. Caragiale sets it in the Wallachia of about 1800.

Dardarot, the king of Hell, is determined to find out what truth there is in the complaint of men who come to Hell, that their wives are to blame for their perdition. He instructs the imp Aghiuţă to go up on earth in the likeness of a man and live with a wife for ten years; then to die and return to Hell with his report.

Aghiuţă takes one hundred thousand ducats from Dardarot's treasury and chooses Bucharest for his work. He has been there often before; it is a good place for amusement; money is scarce ("if you are rich, go to a poor city . . . from every crumb which a poor man tries to raise to his mouth, you snatch more than half"). He acquires a fine house and servants. Knowing that they will be inquisitive, he tells the housekeeper, Kera Marghioala, the following tale:

My name, as I have told you, is Kir Ianulea. I am by origin from the district of Mount Athos. My parents, humble folk, kept themselves by means of a small olive grove. When I was in my seventh year, my parents felt a longing to make a pilgrimage; and so, procuring some money, they took me with them and we went on muleback as far as the port of Salonica. There we boarded a large ship which was waiting with sails spread for a wind, to make southward to Jaffa. Presently the expected wind began to blow, the canvas filled, and we sailed. For three sunny days and nights we kept straight ahead without any trouble. According to the custom we were fasting. About the third day, for our midday meal, we ate beans and radishes. What was the result? Around the time of vespers my parents began to clasp their hands to their bellies and wail horribly: "I'm dying! I'm dying!" The captain, seeing them writhing and curling up in deadly pain, quickly sent for a papist monk who had boarded the vessel with us, a learned man who was skilled in the care of disease. Before the monk arrived, the patients had begun to turn livid and could scarcely tell him what they had eaten—beans and radishes. The monk asked again: "I understand, my children; but you must tell me, did you eat beans and radishes, or radishes and beans?" My mother replied in a faint voice: "Radishes and beans." "Ah, that's bad!" said the monk. And he gave orders to rub their bellies with rough tow. But they rubbed in vain till they took the skin off; for while the moon was rising, first my father and immediately after him my mother passed away. What was I, a child, to do? I followed the captain and the monk around, weeping, and I heard them talking as follows. Said the Captain: "Father, if it's cholera, I'm done for; they won't let me enter port for forty days, and my cargo will be spoiled and I shall be left a poor man." But the learned man replied: "It is no more cholera than I am a nun. It is a sort of disease which rages chiefly among Eastern Christians during Lent. People make a mistake—men are like that, subject to error—they eat radish first and then beans. The radish, you see, directs its strength upward, and the bean exerts its force in the opposite direction; one pushes, the other resists. The struggle begins with great speed in the entrails, spasm after spasm, until there is an entanglement of the bowels and the membrane bursts. Then the patient dies of 'hurduharism'—that is the name the Greeks give to this fearful disease." "Is it infectious?" "Not at all; don't be alarmed."

They wrapped my parents decently in some clean sheets and lit a wax candle at their heads. Another Greek monk read the burial service, and early in the morning, as the sun showed above the waves—"eternal rest"—one! two! three! and they cast them into the deep. Seeing me weeping, the captain took pity on me and made me an apprentice—first as a servant, then as assistant, later as partner. I cannot tell you, dear Kera Marghioala, what miseries I endured, how many oaths, insults, and blows I swallowed; how often I all but perished in the deep; how often circumstances disappointed me and people deceived me—especially after I took a ship for myself and started up in business of my own account, with no master or partner but my own luck. I won't tell you how once I escaped with my life in my bare skin; for after I had been at sea six months I was just about to enter Constantinople, when my ship caught fire with its cargo of tin and amber worth more than two thousand pounds, which I had bought with pepper and dates worth only two hundred. I cannot tell you what I suffered in those distant travels by land and sea from beasts, and worse, from men. Enough to say that little by little, I prospered satisfactorily and ended by having quite a good position. In my travels through the world I have learned polite behavior. I know plenty of foreign languages—at least, as regards Romanian, I can say without boasting that I know it thoroughly; to tell you the truth, although I am of Albanian stock and have not had much book-learning; on this point I yield to no Romanian, be he ever so learned a scholar. I particularly like the language and people of this place, and so, as I have had enough of the dangers of travel and the worries and anxieties of trade, I have come to settle here in Wallachia at Bucharest, to enjoy in peace the fruit of my labors.

He tells the housekeeper to keep this secret under pain of dismissal with a beating; this has the desired result of spreading the story all over the town.

Kir Ianulea's lavish entertainments and pleasant manners make him a much-desired son-in-law. He sets his eye on a beautiful young woman named Acriviţa and easily obtains her father's consent. As soon as the wedding feast is over, she shows her mettle. She intimidates the servants and grows harsh and arrogant to her husband, who only loves her the more. She loses heavily at cards and bursts out when Ianulea mildly protests that they will be bankrupt. Things go from bad to worse. She begins to remove and sell the valuables from the house. She induces him to provide her brothers with capital for trading ventures. Presently his credit becomes shaky. When the news that his brothers-in-law have lost their capital spreads, his creditors decide to keep a watch on him. But he is too quick for them.

At dawn he rose quietly, collected the dregs that remained at the bottom of the money chest, went down to the stable, ordered them to saddle a Tartar ambler, mounted, telling the groom that he was going to Snagov for fresh fish and that he had guests coming to dinner in the evening, went out of the gate at a walk, and then with eyes straining ahead, off we go!

When he turned to the left below the Cathedral toward the Field of Filaret, the light of daybreak was showing, so that as he climbed the hill in front of Cuţitul-de-Argint and looked back downhill, he observed a large group of horsemen apparently galloping after him. His suspicion was in fact well founded. The merchants had found out and had quickly set out after him with policemen from the Agie. He tried to leave the main road and keep to the right under the hill, but he came upon some ditches, and his horse stumbled and threw him. He then picked himself up, abandoned his horse, and set off on foot. He climbed to some palings and vaulted them; then there was another ditch and more fences till, reaching the summit utterly exhausted, he stopped in front of a little vineyard belonging to a squat, fat market gardener who was just giving his eyes a morning bath in the sunshine on the seat outside his shed.

When Kir Ianulea saw him, he said panting:

"Good morning, neighbor; what's your name?"

"Good morning, master; my name's Negoiţă. What's yours?"

"Kir Ianulea."

And his joints scarcely supporting him, he crossed the stile into the vineyard and said:

"Negoiţă, my friend, take pity on me and save me! Some enemies are trying to get their claws into me, to ruin me. Hide me somewhere round here, and I'll make you a rich man. And if I don't prove to you, before I leave here, that I can benefit you, then I agree that you shall hand me over to my enemies. Please, Negoiţă, please, please don't leave me to my destruction."

Negoiţă scratched his head as he thought for a while and then replied:

"Listen to me, Kir Ianulea. Who are your enemies? They aren't boyars, are they? For I tell you frankly, I'm not quarreling with boyars."

"Boyars? Of course not; they're merchants."

"In that case, I'll save you."

Negoiţă hides him and puts the pursuers off the scent. When the coast is clear, Ianulea tells him the whole story of his adventures since leaving the underworld.

"And now, Negoiţă, listen to how I can benefit you. Whenever you hear that the devil has entered into a woman, wife or maid, in whatever place or of whatever stock, you may be sure that it is I. So go there at once; for I shall not come out till you drive me. Naturally, if you heal her, you will not lose by it. The husband or parents, as the case may be, will reward you handsomely. What do you say? Does that suit?"

"Of course!" answered Negoiţă with a smile. And Kir Ianulea, after thanking him once more, went his way.

Less than a month later Negoiţă going down to town with some early cherries for sale, hears of a girl who is possessed by a devil and is uttering all sorts of accusations and revealing secrets.

When Negoiţă heard all this, he sold off his baskets wholesale to the middlemen at whatever price he could get and went straight off to see the possessed girl. When he got there, he made his way through the assembled crowd and told her parents and betrothed that he would save the girl if they would give him a hundred ducats. Naturally the poor people did not wait to think it over; a hundred it should be! And Negoiţă went up to the patient's ear and, pretending to utter an exorcism, said softly and timidly:

"I have come, Kir Ianulea, as we agreed."

"I know," the spirit whispered back, "but to tell you the truth, Negoiţă, I didn't think you so soft as to be content with a hundred ducats! You ought to have asked for big money. But as you have made a mistake, I will forgive you this time. I'm off now to Craiova, to enter into the wife of the Caimacam. Present yourself there next week. Don't keep me waiting too long; I have other business besides looking after you. The Caimacam loves his wife like the eyes in his head; he is rich and generous. This is the last deal, so play your cards well, for thereafter you have no more power over me. You must know that after that I am released from any promise and our partnership is ended!"

Negoiţă takes his hundred ducats and prepares for the journey to Craiova. Arriving there, he learns at an inn of the terrible condition of the Caimacam's wife and the failure of doctors, wise women, and clergy to relieve her. Negoiţă goes quickly to the Caimacam's residence.

A number of ladies and maids were keeping the young woman tied up in sheets, and she was quivering from the top of her head to the soles of her feet. The priests, in great vestments, were holding a service over her and censing her, and her husband was weeping and telling his beads all the time. When suddenly in comes an Albanian and says in a loud voice:

"Your Highness, excuse me! There is a common man here, who has specially come right from Bucharest; he says that he knows how to charm away diseases like Her Highness's and pledges his life that he will heal her at once."

The unhappy man rose, a last hope lighting up his misery with its rays, and cried:

"Let him come in."

When Negoiţă showed himself on the threshold, before anyone could ask him anything, the young woman ceased trembling and ordered them to remove the sheets, as though she were in her right mind and going for a bath. She looked straight at him, began to laugh merrily as at the sight of an old friend long awaited, and signed to him to come nearer, actually calling him by name:

"Welcome, dear Negoiţă! How are you? Pretty well? Come nearer; I've something to tell you, and no one must hear us."

Who could believe his eyes or ears? Negoiţă pushed them all to one side, approached the patient in the manner of a friend and whispered:

"Forgive me, dear, for keeping you waiting, but you've no idea what a hard journey and what a useless horse I had!"

"It's of no consequence," said the spirit very softly, "I'm leaving. Now that I've enriched you, I'm no longer in your debt. So rest assured, friend Negoiţă, that this is your last. Don't let me find you clinging to my tail, or not only will you get nothing, but I shall be angry, and if I'm angry, you may be very sorry. That's all!"

Negoiţă is rewarded with an estate and the rank of a boyar. For three months he lives in comfort and peace. Then he is summoned to Craiova by the Caimacam and told that the daughter of the ruling Prince of Wallachia is possessed, and only Negoiţă can save her. "I'm done for!" thinks Negoiţă, but allows himself to be taken to Bucharest. The Prince and his wife meet him at the head of the palace steps and take him to the sick girl.

There she sat cross-legged on a rug on the floor, shaking her head all the time like a doll with its neck on a wire. She had been like this for five days, with her teeth clenched and without closing her eyes for one moment. When Negoiţă appeared, she stopped shaking her head and began to scream in an access of frenzy:

"Outside! Throw him out! Don't let me set eyes on that swine Negoiţă! Outside! Send for Daddy!"

Negoiţă didn't wait for more. Instead of being angry that he was driven out with abuse, he merely shrugged his shoulders, as much as to say: "Well, if you don't want me. . . !" He turned away to leave. But the mother seized him by the hand, while the Prince approached his daughter:

"Here I am! Here's Daddy!"

"Not you!" screamed the girl, "I didn't call for you. Send for my Daddy!"

"*I* am your Daddy!" said the poor old man, through scalding tears. But the girl screamed even louder:

"No, not you! You're ugly! You go away with Negoiţă! Send for Captain Manoli Ghaiduri; he's my real Daddy!"

Negoiţă persuades the Prince that she must be humored. When Manoli is brought in, she smiles sweetly and asks "Daddy" to cut off Negoiţă's nose and ears and throw him out.

Negoiţă thought: "So that's it, is it? Very well!" Then he turned to the Prince and said:

"Your Highness, let everyone move away, so that I can examine the patient more closely."

They all made way for him, and Negoiţă went straight up to the girl, who was tossing and yelling as loud as she could:

"Outside, Negoiţă! Get outside, you boor!"

But he took no notice of her tantrums and said quietly:

"My dear, I should say you'd better go of your own accord."

The girl yelled worse than ever:

"Outside, Negoiţă!"

"That's what you say, is it? You refuse?"

He tried to take her hand. Then she spat in his face and smacked it so hard that Negoiţă's eyes saw sparks.

He wiped his cheek with his sleeve and, going back to the Prince, said:

"Your Highness, this disease is accompanied by a symptom which I have not met before. That there is no remedy to cure it, I would not say; but by myself I can do nothing for the present. I need help. I have a friend here in Bucharest in the Merchants' Quarter who knows how to cure tonsils and earache; she is the widow of a man who squandered his fortune in extravagance and licentious pleasures. He went bankrupt, ran away, and left his poor innocent wife to starve to death. Her name is Acriviţa, wife of Ianulea and daughter of Hadji Cănuţă."

At these words the young woman suddenly stopped screaming and began to quiver, shaking as though at the height of a fever.

"So I beg Your Highness to order horses to be harnessed at once to bring Madam Ianulea here."

He started to move, but she seized his coat tight and screamed in desperation:

"Wait, Negoiţă!"

And the girl's disease vanishes like a dream. Negoiţă seeks out Acriviţa and gives her one hundred ducats which he says are a debt to Kir Ianulea. He also presents her with the deeds of his old vineyard "out of gratitude that her husband lent him money in time of great need." Then, to free himself once and for all from medical duties, he advises her, as a way of earning money, to go to any place where she hears that the devil has entered into a woman and to drive him out by addressing the patient as if she were meeting her husband. And to Acriviţa's astonishment he quotes the terms of endearment which she habitually used to Ianulea. Negoiţă, after a few days more at court, returns loaded with presents from the Prince and his wife, to his estate.

Presently, away in Bucharest, the Metropolitan laments that one of his nieces has begun to have tantrums. Acrivița hears of it, and on her arrival at his palace, the young woman is instantly cured.

That night Aghiuță returns to Hell, utterly exhausted. Dardarot is highly amused at his report and asks what he wants as a reward.

"Your Darkness, as a reward I shall venture to ask two favors."

"Tell me, dear boy."

"First, that I may never see Acrivița and Negoiță here! Let them go to Heaven, and St. Peter can cope with them as best he may."

"Good. And the second?"

"The second: let me rest at home for a little while; I am worn out with all this business on earth."

"Good again. You have leave to sleep for the next three hundred years, and no one shall bother you with anything."

With these words Dardarot gave him the usual kick and sent him to bed. And so Acrivița and Negoiță went, each at the appointed time, to Heaven; but Aghiuță lay down to sleep . . . and he slept and slept and may be sleeping still, unless he has got up, the imp, to start some more devilries.

Kir Ianulea is a masterly piece of writing, every detail counting for so much—as in that other masterly tale, "La hanul lui Mînjoală"—that it is surprising to look back and see in how few pages the tale has been told. In "Hanul lui Mînjoală" the supernatural element is at work in the comparatively sober setting of a country life not so noticeably different from that which Caragiale knew in his own day. In *Kir Ianulea* the background is much more colorful; it is Wallachia at a time when town life was colored with a Levantine culture developed by Greeks living under Turkish rule. The tale has the charm of a series of aquatints from a travel book of the century before last. And the ironical detachment of Caragiale is at its best. The delicious absurdity of Ianulea's cock-and-bull story of his parents' death, Acrivița's extravagant gossip about her friend, which provokes protest even from her infatuated husband, the malice of the imp in making the possessed princess ask for her "real Daddy"—all these linger in the memory as vivid moments of joyous comedy.

CHAPTER 10

Verses, Parodies, and Other Prose

I *Verses and Parodies*

VERSE forms only a small part of Caragiale's writing. Apart from one or two serious pieces written in his early twenties, it consists of epigrams, fables, and parodies. He started composing fables—Grigore Alexandrescu and other Romanian writers of the nineteenth century had already used the fable for political satire—as part of his reaction to the agrarian revolt of 1907 and its repression; some were published anonymously. The parodies form the most interesting part of his verse. In 1893 he printed several parodies of symbolist poetry of the school of Alexandru Macedonski. A much later parody, "Paşa din Silistra" (The Pasha of Silistra), illustrates his facility of improvisation. In a circle of writers the poet Şt. Iosif wondered how Dimitrie Bolintineanu (1819-73) could have written so many poems. Caragiale then told Iosif to take a sheet of paper and dictated to him a parody of Bolintineanu. "As you see," he said, when "Paşa din Silistra" was completed, "it's not hard; in 25 minutes I write a poem, which means 16 a day, assuming that Bolintineanu worked only six hours daily."[1] The parody is 32 lines long and exactly catches the jog-trot effect of Bolintineanu's heroic poetry.

In a similar spirit in prose he did a parody ("Smărăndiţa") of his friend Barbu Delavrancea's story "Sultănica," making fun of its wealth of adjectives and diminutives and saying that such childish stories were not hard to write.[2] He even treated the theme of his own tale "O făclie de Paşte" in a style of extreme affectation, beginning with a personification of nature in springtime: "Nature, like a ravished bride, who has slept bewitched in the icy chains of a cruel ravishing giant. . . ." In the note introducing the parody he explains ironically that literature is an art which does not have to be learned: anyone who knows how syllables are formed from letters and words from syllables is well enough prepared to practice literature.[3]

II *Literary Articles*

Of his literary articles "Politică şi literatură" (Politics and Literature) is a series of six open letters to the writer Vlahuţă. In the first of these he quotes a passage in which Goethe maintains that a poet is ruined if he devotes himself to politics. Caragiale holds, on the contrary, that there are instances where involvement in political struggles has greatly helped certain poets as poets, citing Dante as an example. In the third letter he rebuts a suggestion of Vlahuţă's that if Eminescu had not died young, he would have entered politics and ceased to write poetry. Caragiale is convinced that success in politics would have increased Eminescu's confidence and made him an even more admirable poet. He then ironically and with some bitterness develops the advice he would have given to Eminescu: to enter the political struggle because otherwise he will live and die in poverty. In the fourth letter he imagines himself at the age of twenty asking Vlahuţă (whom he assumes for the sake of argument to have the experience of life which he possesses now in 1909) for advice about his future career. He concludes that if he had not devoted himself to literature, he might have counted for something in Romania.

What Caragiale has to say about Eminescu is of particular interest. Immediately after the poet's death in 1889, Caragiale wrote the piece "In Nirvana" (To Nirvana), a reminiscence and a characterization of Eminescu, which begins thus:

> It was twenty years ago. In the house where I was living there lodged an actor, who in summer was a theatrical manager in the provinces. The season of actors' migration was over, and those birds of passage were returning to their nests. Seeing that I was continually reading, the actor said to me with a sort of pride: "You like to busy yourself with literature . . . I too have a boy in my company who reads a lot; he's very learned, he reads German, and has great gifts: he writes poems. He wrote us some splendid couplets. I think you'd enjoy meeting him."
>
> And he told me how in a hotel at Giurgiu he had found this boy—who was working in the yard and the stables—lying in the hay and reading Schiller aloud. In the hayrack, on one side, was a suitcase—the boy's library—full of German books. The boy was very gentle and well behaved; he had no vices. He was a stranger from a long way off, he said, but he would not tell where. It was clear he was the son of respectable parents and had reached his present position in some mysterious way. The actor had offered to take him on as prompter at 80 lei a month, and the boy had accepted gladly. He had brought his

library and was now in Bucharest. In the evening he was due to come to the manager—so I should be able to see him.

I was very curious to meet him. I don't know why, but I imagined the young adventurer to be an extraordinary person, a hero, a future great man. In my imagination, seeing him in revolt against the ways of common life, I concluded that this man's contempt for social discipline was a proof that he must be the product of a "de luxe" press, not one of those which turn out stereotyped copies in tens of thousands. Although generally speaking the theory from which I started as premise—namely, that a great man must be in every respect unconventional—was hasty, perhaps even quite unfounded, in this particular case it proved abundantly true.

The young man arrived. He was a delight! A classic face framed in long black tresses: a high clear forehead: large eyes—at those windows of the soul you could see that there was someone inside: a gentle and deeply melancholy smile. He had the air of a young saint who had stepped down from an old icon, a child predestined to pain, on whose face could be read the writing of agonies to come. "My name is Mihail Eminescu." That was how I met him. How we reeled off philosophy to one another all that night with the energy of seventeen years of age! What enthusiasm, what merriment! My imagination had certainly not deceived me. He was a wonderful lad.

One night he introduced me to German literature, which fascinated him. "If you are so fond of poetry," I said, "you must write it too . . . I've been told that you've already written some." "Yes, I have." "Then—I'm fond of poetry too, although I can't write it—be a good chap and show me one of your poems." Eminescu complied at once. It was a piece dedicated to an actress with whom he was very much in love. I can scarcely remember it. I only know that it dealt with the glory and riches of an Assyrian king who was rendered unhappy by a frustrated passion . . . something of that sort. This poem, I think, was published in No. 68 or 69 of *Familia* [The Family] in Budapest.

Next day we met again. But meanwhile a private unhappiness had intervened. The actress had been very little moved by the sorrows of the Assyrian king. This time Eminescu was silent and gloomy; he spoke very little, and contradiction irritated him. In vain did I beg him to show me another poem, or reread me the one I already knew. He went to bed early, and next day at noon, when I went to see him, I found him still asleep. I roused him. His ill-humor had now passed off; in fact, he was even merrier than two days before. We spent the whole day laughing; he talked to me about ancient India, about the Dacians, about Stephen the Great, and he sang me the *doina*. The Assyrian king's pique had passed, and he was now enjoying his wealth and glory.

That was how I knew him then; that was how he remained until his last good moments: merry and sad; communicative and morose; gentle and rough; contented to live on nothing and always discontented with everything; now abstinent as a hermit, now again greedy for the pleasures of life; fleeing men and seeking them; impassive as an old Stoic and irritable as a girl with nerves. A strange mixture–lucky for an artist, unfortunate for a man!

In the following month Caragiale published "Ironie" (Irony), in which he rebutted the notion that Eminescu had not lived in poverty. When these articles were reprinted in 1892 in the volume *Note şi schiţe*, Caragiale added touches to "Ironie" which made it offensive to Maiorescu, and printed a new piece, "Două note" (Two Notes), in which he accused Maiorescu of mutilating the text of poems and insinuated that he was making a profit from his edition of them. This attack, followed by the lecture at the Ateneu in which he ridiculed *Junimea*, caused the breach between Caragiale and Maiorescu, which Caragiale was in the end to regret.

In another open letter to Vlahuţă from a later section of the series mentioned above, a section called "Morală şi educaţie" (Morals and Education), Caragiale, rebutting the charge that the Romanians are a depraved people and maintaining that they are only an unformed one, implies in a short passage that they have something original to contribute in literature.

The Romanians today are a people of over ten million souls in all, with one and the same language, which (boasting aside) is extraordinarily beautiful and . . . difficult, and with a distinct mode of thought of its own, a priceless treasure of moral philosophy, humor, and poetry–a possession all the more original for being a medley of ancient inheritances and acquisitions–Greek, Slavonic, Oriental, and other–all stamped with its undeniable seal of nobility, a Romance, Latin seal, which proves it their true and undeniable owner. From this age-old possession stems this nation's unbeaten power of assimilation: it is only just beginning remotely to feel its importance in the European world.

This makes explicit something which shows in Caragiale's work and especially in his later fiction, that unlike many influential writers of nineteenth-century Romania, he did not repudiate the non-Romance elements in the Romanian language and culture; he relished them because they gave it an original flavor.

III *Political Articles*

Of the political articles, "1907" must be singled out as the most renowned. Caragiale wrote it from his retirement at Berlin, deeply moved by the terrible events of that year in Romania. It is by no means a partisan piece; Caragiale's judgment is pronounced far from all political parties. The following passage on the shortcomings of the Romanian educational system gives a sample of the writer's eloquence:

> All the schools from the humblest to the universities–primary schools, secondary, professional, agricultural, commercial, theological, schools of midwifery, music and other arts, faculties of all the branches of higher education–all give their graduates more or less indiscriminately rights to public dignities and positions. Thus, the Romanian schools, instead of being a means for educating the people and the governing classes, become a pipe channeling the citizens' lust for first place, for easy social climbing, for exemption from dues, for increase of rights and privileges. More and more, from the lowest to the highest grade, the schools are factories for producing officials, civil servants, and lawyers–a plethora of half-educated persons without character or humanity, veritable intellectual sharpers, whose only need is the maximum of honors without any desert and of gain without much effort.
>
> These factories supply the public oligarchy which is in exclusive control of Romania. From them the oligarchy of adventurers emerges and is renewed and grows in the blind struggle of competition for rank, distinction, and profit. Year by year in the public arena there appear in theatrical poses the theoreticians, the reformers and patriots, the placid inventors of new systems, the heady agitators, chauvinists, nationalists, irredentists, anti-Semites, xenophobes, each riding his warhorse to outstrip the rest, to the naïve amusement of the idle plebs, the handmaid of oligarchy. The poor families of the urban plebs, lacking any means of production, living by petty trade or on minor official posts or as local publicans or by trades less readily acknowledged–all aspire, thanks to the national schools, to see their children, as soon as possible after coming of age, at the worst, public servants; at best, members of Parliament capable of becoming ministers if not actually so. And as in the wildest lotteries, so here, not all illusions are disappointed.

As a sample of his few political speeches, here is the opening of the one delivered at Jassy on behalf of Take Ionescu's Conservative-Democrat party in 1908 as reported by the press:[4]

Gentlemen,

One fine summer evening, a young traveler, wearied with journeying, arrived by a spring and sat down to rest. Below to the west there rose in front of him an ancient forest, and behind the forest the sun was going down in splendor.

His weariness combined with the lofty beauty of the prospect to cast a spell on him . . . and beneath their spell our young wayfarer sank into a deep sleep. He sank into a deep sleep . . . and slept very well. When he awoke—the next morning—the sun was rising. In front of the youth to the west the sun no longer lit up the ancient forest behind which it had set last night . . . it lit up a stately city: with palaces, cathedrals, towers, cupolas, and viaducts and the movement and noise of a great city. Instead of last night's black forest, what a magic vision of the air appeared beneath the clear brilliance of morning! The man wiped his eyes in amazement. Impossible! "Impossible! I went to sleep last night, I'm sure, in front of a forest, and now when I wake up. . . ."

And disbelieving his own eyes, he bent over the spring to wash them . . . and looking at himself in the water the young man of last night saw himself this morning with a long white beard down to his waist. He had slept for a hundred years. Naturally the old man was left petrified.

Well, just so have people here been left petrified when, after sleeping for half a century, they have found themselves faced with the recent social and political events. The boyar wipes his eyes in the morning, when he awakes and is faced with the work of time, with such a profound change in the world. The boyar is left amazed when in front of his uplifted pipe, instead of humble submission, he encounters a man who tells him: "It seems to me, sir, that you don't perceive reality and that you can no longer reason clearly." Just as the man in the story was amazed at the city which had appeared miraculously, many people in this country were amazed at the peasants' revolution. Yes, we must give things their proper names—it was a revolution—not a revolt.

The disturbance of public order at a certain time and place, even when it is logical, is a revolt; but the general rising of a whole world, even when it seems to have no logic, is a revolution.

Just as here Caragiale uses his gift of narration to fix the attention of his hearers, so at the beginning of another speech in the same campaign he catches them with phrases that will remind them of the election meeting in *O scrisoare pierdută.*[5]

IV *Correspondence*

The surviving letters written by Caragiale are in general interesting as biographical documents rather than as belles-lettres. The letters to intimate friends such as Petre Missir, Alceu Urechia, and Paul Zarifopol are, as we should expect, lively and full of private jokes. One letter, however, stands out from the rest as being as much a work of art as his best comic sketches, and all the more pungent and outspoken for being written not for the public, but for a close friend of all parties concerned. It is a very long letter to Alceu Urechia in July, 1905, describing how Caragiale showed Barbu Delavrancea the sights of Berlin.[6]

Sometimes his letters express his views on personalities in a trenchant form. Thus, when Mihai Dragomirescu tells him that, having been replaced as editor of *Convorbiri literare*, he has broken with Maiorescu, and uses the phrase "The divorce took place the day before yesterday," Caragiale replies congratulating him on the "divorce": "I was sure that the affair would end like that. In the end, the honorable young innocent was bound to open his eyes and see what a sham the tarted-up old procuress was. . . ."[7]

In strong contrast to this tone is a letter written at about the same time to the Socialist writer, C. Dobrogeanu-Gherea.[8] Caragiale wants to persuade Gherea to come with his family to Berlin for a rest cure. Gherea must refresh himself with "another sort of sport than that of doing your duty in such an unrewarding field" (i.e., preaching socialism in Romania). "I know how passionately keen you are on this humanitarian and social sport; so I should not be capable of joking with you on this point, and I hasten to state (I, a man incapable of any other sport than contemplation) that from all points of view I consider your sport the only one (after my own) worthy of a man of sound mind." But no sport must be overdone; strain must be relaxed. After a formal exposition of the argument that altruism must not mean the complete annihilation of egoism but a well-balanced compromise with it, Caragiale goes on: "We have known one another for some time, dear Costică; you have had long enough to realize how little I should be capable of wounding anyone in his beliefs and enthusiasms, when I see them to be noble and know them to be sincere and honorable. You of all people, one of the very few men (not to say the only one) whom I have met in our country with a sincere and honorable belief—how could I wound you? If I sometimes jest, I think you realize that I am not jesting about the belief, but about the sham believers, whose public career I long ago foretold to you. You have realized, I hope, how right I was when I once said to you in jest, that you had made many Socialists in Romania and not been able to keep one. I am the only one you could not make into a Socialist, and I am the only one who remains faithful to you and will continue so—although you consider me 'bourgeois, reactionary, etc.'—all Socialist terms of abuse, to which an anarchist like myself pays no attention." After which he teases Gherea for his "legalism" and pleads the superiority of anarchism and terrorist methods! This letter is a remarkable blend of irony with serious concern and a sensitive tact which was by no means an obvious characteristic of Caragiale.

CHAPTER 11

The Man

TO begin with the less attractive aspects of Caragiale's personality, there is the violence which erupted from time to time in his life and which is reflected in his work, especially in what he wrote between 1880 and 1895. The blows which the errand boy Cănuţă received from his angry employer in "Cănuţă om sucit" (Canutza, an Awkward Customer) and which the hero of "Norocul culegătorului" (The Compositor's Luck) also suffered had been dealt out in reality by the young Caragiale as proofreader in a newspaper office to the compositors whose errors infuriated him.[1] If the smashing of the pink plates by Lefter Popescu in "Două loturi" was not mere autobiography, Caragiale's daughter at least implies that similar scenes did occur in the life of the family.[2]

There was also a streak of malice, which took at times such forms as the cruel and tiresome practical joke which, when director of the National Theater, he played on the actress Frosa Sarandy.[3] At other times it might have an artistic motive as well, as when he would exasperate the Hungarian market women at Braşov, so as afterward to amuse his friends with mimicry of their accents.[4]

For Caragiale's wit to be at its most splendid, says a friend, he had to be worked up against someone or something.[5] No doubt there was splendor if his artistry was in control; but there were occasions when, even though unprovoked, he did not control his speech. Iacob Negruzzi advances as one of the reasons why the meetings of *Junimea* after its move from Jassy to Bucharest were less enjoyable than before—the presence of ladies—for in the presence of ladies, he says, "it was too painful for a young author to find himself criticized, and when Caragiale with his cutting speech and ruthless character exploded some youth reading his own composition, with a stinging remark that was far from polite in expression, an uncomfortable feeling suddenly spread through the gathering."[6] In a bad humor Caragiale would turn his sarcasm even on the customers of his own brasserie.[7]

To illustrate his irrational fear of fire and of heights, two anecdotes may be quoted. At a performance of Wagner's *Rheingold* he could not bear the flickering flames of the smithy in the third scene and dragged his son Matei from the opera house.[8] When persuaded to walk in the mountains round Sinaia, he was so overcome by the sight of a precipice that he could only be induced to move when blindfolded and led by hand.[9] His obsessional fears for his children's health, though exaggerated, had a rational basis: the loss of his first two little girls in 1892.

Other characteristics were his restlessness and improvidence. Not only did he move house frequently in Bucharest, but even when settled in Berlin, he would transfer the members of the family from one room to another. As his daughter said: "Father liked change, and quickly tired of the same decor."[10] The family suffered also from shortage of money. This was in part due to Caragiale giving priority over household needs, when money did come his way, to making merry with his friends.

His friendships were often tested nearly to breaking point by his unwillingness to repay, when in funds, the loans which his friends had advanced in moments of crisis.[11] Nevertheless the fact that he was nearly always forgiven shows the value put upon his friendship. It was not merely that—except when out of humor—he was extraordinarily good company. His friends were willing to put up with much because they loved and esteemed the man. On the whole he chose as friends men who enjoyed the same Bohemian atmosphere as he himself, regardless whether they were intellectuals or not. In fact, in his study of humanity achieved through casual contacts he was less interested in intellectuals than in simple folk.[12]

Writing of Eminescu, Caragiale said: "When a passion seized him, it was an extraordinary torture."[13] His own relation with women was quite different; the detachment which makes him a great comic writer enabled him to view the relationship more coolly.[14] When he finally married, he showed himself a good husband and father, as he had been a good son and brother. There was a strong current of emotion in him; he was right, when on one occasion he was referred to as a humorist, to protest that on the contrary he was a profoundly emotional man.[15] He is recorded as bursting into tears when he heard of Eminescu's mental breakdown and when he saw the daughter of his friend Delavrancea dangerously ill.[16] This emotionalism underlying his detachment may account for what one friend noted in him: often, he says, Caragiale would be enthusiastic about some new acquaintance, only to pass rapidly to an exaggerated contempt for that person.[17]

His love of classical music is unexpected in a man brought up as he was in a country which in his youth had little tradition of orchestral or chamber music. Friends have recorded his observations on his favorite composers–Bach, Mozart, Beethoven, Brahms–as well as on Wagner, about whose music he had mixed feelings. Chopin and César Franck were not at all to his taste. In spite of his view that the true esthetic attitude was one of contemplation with strong emotion excluded, he was seen with tears in his eyes during the choral movement of Beethoven's Ninth Symphony.[18] Once again his appreciation of form in art was accompanied by an underlying emotionalism.

Caragiale's political attitudes are a problem which has received considerable attention.[19] In youth he sympathized with the Liberals, the more progressive of the two political parties of those times. He has given an amusing description in *Boborul* of his part in the attempted coup d'état in 1870, when Captain Al. Candiano-Popescu proclaimed a republic at Ploeşti. The newspapers for which he worked in the years 1874-77 were Liberal. When in 1878 he entered the literary circle of *Junimea*, he found himself in a milieu where Liberal ideas were subjected to rigorous criticism. Nevertheless, though he worked for some months with Eminescu on the Conservative paper *Timpul*, he never became a member of Junimea's political group. The posts which he held in the 1880's in the inspectorate of schools, in the tobacco factory, and in the state monopolies were all given him by Liberal ministers, and in 1885 he contributed to the official Liberal organ *Voinţa naţională* (The National Will). When the Conservatives came to power in 1888, he applied to Maiorescu, now minister of education, for the directorship of the National Theater. Maiorescu was unwilling to grant his request on the ground that Caragiale was temperamentally unfit to manage a company of actors, but eventually yielded to persuasion by Queen Elizabeth.[20]

After his resignation as director, Caragiale seems to have expected his Junimist friends in the government to procure him a pension on which he could devote himself entirely to literature. This he was told was without precedent.[21] This failure, together with his resentment at being treated, as he felt, by the Junimist leaders as a social inferior, caused his final alienation from *Junimea*, marked by his public lecture at the Ateneu in which he attacked the group. In that year he drew closer to the Socialists. The Romanian Socialist movement had taken shape in Jassy about 1878; its chief, Ioan Nădejde, moved to Bucharest in 1893.[22] One of Caragiale's best friends was C. Dobrogeanu-Gherea, literary critic and exponent of Socialist theory. Nevertheless, Caragiale's antipathy to "form without content" made him as critical of the Socialists as of the Liberals. "You Socialists" he burst out once "are only men of phrases!"[23] But the chief opponents of "form without content," the Junimist section of the Conservatives, annoyed him by their social pretensions. It was therefore not surprising that he was attracted in 1895 to join a new Radical-Democrat party, created by G. Panu, an ex-Junimist, who wanted universal suffrage and agrarian reform. However, it soon melted away; in 1896 Panu and some of his supporters including Caragiale joined the Conservative party led by Lascar Catargi, which did not include the Junimists. For the Conservative paper *Epoca* Caragiale wrote political leaders in 1896 and 1897.

From 1901 he had no political allegiance till 1907, when he joined the new Conservative-Democrat party, described by its founder Take Ionescu as "democratic in composition, progressive in tendency—firmly representing the ideas of social conservation." Caragiale was by this time settled in Berlin, but he actually went to Romania to take part in his chief's campaign. He hoped for some time to be nominated as candidate at some by-election, but this never happened, and before his death his enthusiasm for the party chief had waned.[24]

Clearly Caragiale was temperamentally unsuited to be a politician. He was not a party man; he was an individualist, and he was too vividly conscious of the weaknesses in the program of any party whose cause he might have espoused. Before he became a man of private means, his flirtations with political parties were largely motivated by the hope of being given some undemanding post which would enable him to devote a large part of his time to writing. But his activity—during his later life as a rentier—on behalf of Take Ionescu's Conservative-Democrats was disinterested; he was provoked to political activity by the agrarian troubles of 1907 and their repression.

In his political attitudes we see the generous impulses of a reformer controlled by the critical attitude typical of *Junimea*, the rejection of "form without content"; in his attitude as a creator we shall see something of a parallel—strong emotion mastered and partly concealed by a will to give the most perfect form to his creations.

CHAPTER 12

The Artist

THERE is plenty of testimony to the fascination of Caragiale's talk. It lay partly in his gift for mimicry. "You could tell he was from a family of actors–he could talk like a Greek, a Jew, a Transylvanian, a Moldavian, Kogălniceanu, Dumitru Brătianu–you would have sworn it was they themselves both in their way of thinking and their manner of talking."[1] This was what made him such a splendid reader of his own comedies.[2] But in addition to mimicry he had a wonderful gift of improvisation and was peculiarly inspired in congenial company. At a dinner on the eve of a public meeting in Jassy which he was to address on behalf of Take Ionescu's political campaign, he was persuaded to tell the company what he proposed to say in public the next day. According to Eugen Herovanu: "The speech on the previous evening had attained the peaks of inspiration and art; the second one could not equal it." The same writer comments that "Caragiale seems as a talker in an intimate circle, especially *inter pocula*, to have achieved beauties of construction, language, thought, imagination and wit, superior to his written work."[3] Those close to him regretted that so much was never committed to paper. "He would spend the night in telling stories and reel off new sketches to the delight of all, and then would neglect to write them down."[4]

Caragiale sometimes denied that he had talent. (He used the word to mean a "natural gift" and not in opposition to "genius"). "I'm clever, but I've no talent." Or more reasonably, "I've got along more by intelligence than by talent."[5] He was certainly right to stress the part played by intelligence and application in his writing. For him it was very hard work, as his daughter has described it.

It is well known that father wrote with difficulty. He himself often said so. In particular the beginnings were difficult; he passed through veritable crises, in which distrust alternated with optimism. We used to see him emerging agitatedly from his room with drawn face, obviously dissatisfied, cursing his unhappy profession and the abominable thought that he had ever taken it up, and he would counsel us never to follow his example but to choose any other profession. "For" he would add "better be a good cobbler than a bad writer." But he also used to tell us that he wrote because it was a compulsion stronger than his will. At other times, after retiring angrily into what he called his "torture chamber," he would reappear after some time in a good humor, and begin to tell us the plan of the work which he wanted to put on paper.

Everything which distracted him from his intense concentration put him into a state of acute irritation. Days passed without food and nights without rest. We would hear him walking agitatedly about his room. My bed was against a hidden door which led into his room. He coughed a great deal and the wave of smoke from the cigarettes which he lit one after the other would filter under the door between us. A state of oppressive disquiet reigned in the house; we all went about on tiptoe, doors were closed noiselessly, no laughter rang out, and conversation was whispered. "Quiet, father's working." Till suddenly, at a single word, we all brightened. The door would open and father would appear with a familiar gleam on his tired face: "It's going, it's going well!"

But this did not mean the end of his toil. He went on writing, and after finishing a page, he would tear it up because of some detail or other, sometimes a single word. And patiently he would start again. This he called "brushing," and again it lasted for whole days and nights of hesitations, reconsiderations, continuous trials, down to the last comma, with the same conscientiousness, the same tireless scrupulosity, until perfection was attained.[6]

Nor was this confined to his creative writing. An observer has described "with what difficulty and scrupulosity Caragiale wrote the political articles which he sent to the journal *Epoca*; he was continually writing, erasing and correcting, then rereading, tearing up the page and beginning again. But when after much effort he gave them their final form, making a fair copy in his beautiful handwriting, the article was an artistic jewel; thought, images, and style perfect."[7] He would even treat a telegram or a postcard with as much care as a literary composition.[8] No wonder, then, that he was continually worrying editors about proof correction; his "erratophobia" was obsessive.

He prided himself on his knowledge of Romanian and would say: "Not many are masters of it as I am."[9] His task, in his view, was to search for the perfect expression of what he wanted to say; he observed, incidentally, that the final solution was always shorter than the preceding versions.[10] "A word" he said "can have only one place in a sentence. And if you don't know how to put it there, the entire sentence collapses, like a building in which a single block of stone has been wrongly placed."[11] For all this preoccupation with expression, Caragiale was far from overrating form at the expense of content. In a notice which he wrote on the publication of a book of humorous sketches he pointed to an oddity of Romanian literature in his time, that three-quarters of what was written was verse. This he explained on the ground that the technique of verse is easier than that of prose; even without much thought in it, verse would appear respectable provided it was written competently. But if prose lacked thought, it revealed itself as valueless. "Furthermore, it is precisely for the man who thinks and therefore has something to say, that the technique of prose conceals hundreds and thousands of secrets, whose subtlety would defy the most complex course of rhetoric."[12]

We have noted (p. 72) that Caragiale was very sparing in descriptions of scenery. The critic Eugen Lovinescu drew attention to this in an article in Mihai Dragomirescu's journal *Convorbiri* (November 15, 1907). Caragiale, in a private letter to Dragomirescu, made the following defense: "You accuse me of not having in my writings enough love of landscape, of still life, or enough lyricism. I think (not that I want to contradict you systematically) that I may not have too much, very much or much of all these, but I think that I have enough; and I also think that in art what is more than *enough* ought not be there *at all*." He goes on to say that nature and the lyrical are the object of other arts and are only ancillary to the art of storytelling.[13]

As one might expect from a playwright, Caragiale used a great deal of dialogue in his tales and sketches. Instead of explaining the psychological processes of his characters, he lets them reveal themselves in dialogue. This economy in description is stimulating to the reader's imagination and has a similar fascination to that of Evelyn Waugh's fiction. Caragiale once advised a writer of satirical verse not to italicize his points. "Why do you underline the words on whose effect you rely? Is it that you want to open the eyes of readers who are fools? . . . Let me tell you, my dear chap, that witticisms are not for fools. And take it from me that it's not a good idea when you're writing something, to have in mind that you're writing for fools."[14]

The essential tension in Caragiale's art between the fluency of his improvisation and the laborious economy of his writing has been summed up by Vlahuţă in the phrase: "He needed a stenographer and God partnered him with a stone-carver."[15]

Notes and References

Chapter One

1. "Politică şi literatură" (Politics and Literature), *Opere* (Works), IV (Bucharest, 1939), 236–37; *Opere*, ed. Al. Rosetti et al., IV (Bucharest, 1965), 475–76.

2. It seems impossible to translate this title satisfactorily into English; the word has an archaic flavor and the double meaning (a) "false accusation" (b) "disaster."

3. Ecaterina Logadi, "Din amintirile mele despre tată" (From My Memoriés of Father), *Viaţa românească* (Romanian Life), XV, 6 (Bucharest, June 1962), 154–55.

Chapter Two

1. T. Maiorescu, *Însemnări zilnice* (Daily Notes), ed. I. Rădulescu-Pogoneanu, I (Bucharest, n.d.), 294.

2. *Ibid.*, p. 318.

3. *Opere*, ed. P. Zarifopol, I (Bucharest, 1930) p. 311–12.

4. *Corespondenţa dintre I. L. Caragiale şi Paul Zarifopol* (Correspondence between I. L. Caragiale and Paul Zarifopol), ed. Ş. Cioculescu (Bucharest, 1935), p. 72. See also N. Vătămanu and Ş. Cioculescu in *Gazeta literară* (The Literary Gazette), IV, 25 (Bucharest, June 20, 1957).

5. T. Maiorescu, *op. cit.*, p. 329.

6. T. Maiorescu, "Comediile lui I. L. Caragiale" (The Comedies of I. L. Caragiale) in *Convorbiri literare* (Literary Conversations), XIX, 6 (Bucharest, September 1, 1885).

7. *Opere*, ed. Ş. Cioculescu, VI (Bucharest, 1939), p. xvii.

8. I. Negruzzi, *Amintiri din Junimea* (Memories of Junimea), quoted in I. L. Caragiale, *Opere*, ed. Al. Rosetti et al., I (Bucharest, 1959), 749.

Chapter Three

1. T. Maiorescu, *Însemnări zilnice*, ed. I. Rădulescu-Pogoneanu, II (Bucharest, n.d.), 264, 269.

2. I. Suchianu, *Diverse amintiri şi însemnări* (Various Memories and Notes) (Bucharest, 1933), p. 26.

3. "On the Artificial Comedy of the Last Century," *The Works of Charles Lamb*, ed. T. Hutchinson (London, 1924), p. 651.

Chapter Four

1. *Opere*, ed. Al. Rosetti et al., I (Bucharest, 1959), 635–37.
2. *Opere*, ed. Ş. Cioculescu, VI (Bucharest, 1939), xxx-xxxiii. The outline has now been printed by C. Grosu from a MS at the Museum of Romanian Literature, Bucharest, in the museum's quarterly journal *Manuscriptum*, II, 2(3) (Bucharest, 1971), 150–66.

Chapter Five

1. *Opere*, ed. Al. Rosetti et al., I (Bucharest, 1959), 660–61.
2. Quoted *ibid.*, p. 662.
3. Ş. Cioculescu, *Viaţa lui I. L. Caragiale* (The Life of I. L. Caragiale), ed. II (Bucharest, 1969), p. 262.
4. Sofia Nădejde, quoted in *Opere*, ed. Al. Rosetti et al., I (Bucharest, 1959), p. 670.

Chapter Six

1. *Opere*, ed. P. Zarifopol, II (Bucharest, 1931), xxxiv–xxxvi.

Chapter Seven

1. See R. Hingley, *Chekhov: A Biographical and Critical Study* (London, 1950), pp. 35–36.
2. *Opere*, ed. P. Zarifopol, II (Bucharest, 1931), xvii.

Chapter Eight

1. This was pointed out by G. Dăianu, "Izvorul povestirii Abu Hasan a lui I. L. Caragiale" (The Source of I. L. Caragiale's Story Abu Hasan), *Revista fundaţiilor regale* (Review of the Royal Foundations), VIII, II (Bucharest, [1941]), 433–44. The French text is to be found in A. Galland, *Les mille et une nuits* VI (Paris, 1826), 84–212.

Chapter Nine

1. First printed in *Viaţa românească* (Romanian Life), Jassy, XV (November, 1909), 208.

Chapter Ten

1. *Opere*, ed. Al. Rosetti et al., III (Bucharest, 1962), 830–31.
2. *Ibid.*, pp. 708–9.
3. The parody is entitled *Noaptea învierii* (Easter Eve). First printed in his volume of sketches, *Schiţe uşoare* (Light Sketches), (Bucharest, 1896); reprinted in *Opere*, ed. Al. Rosetti et al., III (Bucharest, 1962), 85.

4. Reported in *Ordinea* (Order) (Bucharest, March 9, 1908). Reprinted in *Opere*, ed. Ş. Cioculescu, V (Bucharest, 1938), 221.

5. Reported in *Ordinea* (Bucharest, April 13, 1908). Reprinted in *Opere*, ed. Ş. Cioculescu, V (Bucharest, 1938), 230.

6. *Ion Luca Caragiale: Scrisori şi acte* (Ion Luca Caragiale: Letters and Documents), ed. Ş. Cioculescu (Bucharest, 1963), pp. 19–29.

7. *Ibid.*, p. 43.

8. *Opere*, ed. Ş. Cioculescu, VII (Bucharest, 1942), 253–58.

Chapter Eleven

1. Al. Ionescu, "Caragiale corector" (Caragiale as Proof-Corrector), in *Zeflemeaua* (Banter), Bucharest, I, 23 (March 3, 1902), quoted by Ş. Cioculescu, *Viaţa lui I. L. Caragiale* (The Life of I. L. Caragiale) (Bucharest, 1969), p. 86.

2. Ecaterina Logadi, "Din amintirile mele despre tată" (From My Memories of Father), in *Viaţa românească* (Romanian Life), XV, 6 (Bucharest, June, 1962), 155.

3. Archibald (pseudonym of G. Rădulescu), *Ce am văzut în România mică* (What I Saw in Little Romania) (Bucharest, 1926), pp. 77–83.

4. Cella Delavrancea, "Cîteva amintiri despre Caragiale" (Some Memories of Caragiale), in *Viaţa românească*, XV, 6 (Bucharest, June, 1962), 188.

5. I. D. Gherea, "I. L. Caragiale" in *Viaţa românească*, XV, 6 (Bucharest, June, 1962), 180.

6. I. Negruzzi, *Amintiri din Junimea* (Bucharest, n.d.), p. 286.

7. B. Brănişteanu, "Din amintirile unui vechi gazetar" (From the Memories of an Old Journalist), in *Viaţa românească*, XV, 6 (Bucharest, June 1962), 196.

8. I. D. Gherea, *op. cit.*, p. 178.

9. E. Logadi, *op. cit.*, p. 155.

10. *Ibid.*, p. 154.

11. I. Suchianu, *Diverse însemnări şi amintiri* (Bucharest, 1933), p. 90.

12. E. Logadi, *op. cit.*, p. 159.

13. "In Nirvana," *Opere*, ed. P. Zarifopol, III (Bucharest, 1932), 4.

14. Cf. the love affair described by Ş. Cioculescu, *Viaţa lui I. L. Caragiale* (Bucharest, 1969), pp. 125–34.

15. V. Eftimiu, "Recapitulări" (Recapitulations), in *Viaţa românească*, XV, 6 (Bucharest, June, 1962), 176.

16. T. Maiorescu, *Însemnări zilnice* (Daily Notes), ed. I. Rădulescu-Pogoneanu, II (Bucharest, n.d.), 191; C. Delavrancea, *op. cit.*, p. 187.

17. I. D. Gherea, *op. cit.*, p. 179.

18. *Ibid,*, pp. 178–80; C. Delavrancea, *op. cit.*, p. 188.

19. Caragiale's political attitudes are discussed by Ş. Cioculescu, "Caragiale şi politică" (Caragiale and Politics) in *Revista fundaţiilor regale* (Review of the Royal Foundations), II, 10 (Bucharest, October, 1936). For his activities as journalist, see *Id. Viaţa lui I. L. Caragiale* (Bucharest, 1969), p. 83–112.

20. I. Suchianu, *Diverse însemnări şi amintiri* (Bucharest, 1933), p. 28, quoted in Ş. Cioculescu, *Viaţa lui I. L. Caragiale* (Bucharest, 1969), pp. 167–68.

21. I. E. Torouţiu, *Studii şi documente literare* (Literary Studies and Documents), VII (Bucharest, 1936), 270–71.

22. Eugen Herovanu, *Oraşul amintirilor* (The City of Memories) (Bucharest, 1937), pp. 152 and 163.

23. C. Săteanu, *Caragiale în anecdotă la a 25-a aniversare a morţii sale* (Caragiale in Anecdote on the 25th Anniversary of His Death) (Bucharest, 1937), p. 27.

24. E. Herovanu, *op. cit.*, p. 271; C. Săteanu, *op. cit.*, p. 22.

Chapter Twelve

1. I Suchianu, *Diverse însemnări şi amintiri* (Bucharest, 1933), p. 53. See also E. Logadi, "Din amintirile mele despre tată," in *Viaţa românească*, XV, 6 (Bucharest, June, 1962), 159.

2. I. Negruzzi, *Amintiri din Junimea* (Bucharest, n.d.), p. 286.

3. E. Herovanu, *Oraşul amintirilor* (Bucharest, 1937), pp. 274–77.

4. C. Delavrancea, "Cîteva amintiri despre Caragiale," in *Viaţa românească*, XV, 6 (Bucharest, June, 1962), 189.

5. E. Logadi, *op. cit.*, p. 159.

6. *Ibid,*, p. 157.

7. D. Hogea, *Din trecutul oraşului Piatra-Neamţ, Amintiri* (From the Past of the Town of Piatra-Neamţ, Memories) (Bucharest, 1936), pp. 224–28. See also B. Brănisteanu, "Din amintirile unui vechi gazetar" in *Viaţa românească*, SV, 6 (Bucharest, June, 1962), 194.

8. E. Logadi, *op. cit.*, p. 159.

9. *Ibid.*

10. I. D. Gherea, "I. L. Caragiale," in *Viaţa românească*, XV, 6 (Bucharest, June 1962), p. 181.

11. C. Săteanu, *Caragiale în anecdotă la a 25-a aniversare a morţii sale* (Bucharest, 1937), p. 31.

12. "O bună lectură" in *Opere*, ed. Ş. Cioculescu, IV (Bucharest, 1938), 413.

13. *I. L. Caragiale: Scrisori şi acte*, ed. Ş. Cioculescu (Bucharest, 1963), p. 67.

14. E. Herovanu, *op. cit.*, p. 268.

15. Al. Vlahuţă, *Scrieri alese* (Selected Works), ed. V. Rîpeanu, II (Bucharest, 1963), 521.

Selected Bibliography

PRIMARY SOURCES

Editions:

1. Complete Works

The definitive edition of Caragiale's works was begun by Paul Zarifopol, who published:

Vol. I. *Nuvele şi schiţe*, 1930.
Vol. II. *Nuvele şi schiţe*, 1931,
Vol. III. *Reminiscenţe şi note critice*, 1932,

all with the imprint of the publishing house *Cultura Natională*.

The series was continued by Şerban Cioculescu with the imprint of *Fundaţia pentru literatură şi artă Regele Carol II*:

Vol. IV. *Notiţe critice, literatură şi versuri*, 1938,
Vol. V. *Articole politice şi cronici dramatice*, 1938.
Vol. VI. *Teatru*, 1939,
Vol. VII. *Corespondenţă*, 1942.

This edition reprinted much that had remained buried in periodicals. Its notes are almost entirely confined to textual questions. There are interesting introductions by the respective editors.

The correspondence in Vol. VII of this edition has since been supplemented by Şerban Cioculescu, *I. L. Caragiale: Scrisori şi acte*, 1963.

2. Annotated edition

The edition published under the joint editorship of Al. Rosetti, Ş. Cioculescu, and Liviu Călin, with the imprint of *Editura de stat pentru literatură şi artă*, does not aim at completeness, but has notes which go beyond textual problems.

Vol. I. *Teatru*, 1959,
Vol. II. *Momente, Schiţe, Notiţe critice*, 1960,
Vol. III. *Nuvele, Povestiri, Amintiri, Versuri, Parodii, Varia*, 1962,

Vol. IV. *Publicistică*, 1965.
This edition reclassifies Caragiale's works, the classification in the definitive edition being unsatisfactory. Vol. I contains an introduction by Silvian Iosifescu.

Translations:

1. Plays
Four of the comic plays are translated by Frida Knight, *"The Lost Letter" and other plays by I. L. Caragiale* (London, 1956). The three others are "Carnival Scenes," "A Stormy Night," and "Mr. Leonida and the Reactionaries."
A manuscript in the Museum of Romanian Literature at Bucharest, containing *Năpasta* translated by Lucy Byng under the title "Retribution" is recorded by H. Oprescu, *Scriitori în lumina documentelor* (Bucharest, 1968), p. 59.

2. Stories
Very few of the stories have been translated into English. Versions include "The Inn" ("La conac") in *The Slavonic and East European Review*, XXV, 65 (April, 1947), 325–30, and "Retribution" ("O reparaţie") in *The Slavonic and East European Review*, XXIX, 73 (June, 1951), 372–74, both by Mabel Nandriş; also "Manjoala's Inn" ("La hanul lui Mînjoală") in *Introduction to Romanian Literature*, ed. J. Steinberg (New York, 1966), pp. 20–28.

3. Articles
A translation by E. D. Tappe of part of "1907" has been printed under the title "Causes of the Peasant Revolt, 1907" in *Contrasts in Emerging Societies*, ed. D. Warriner (London, 1965), pp. 200–203.

SECONDARY SOURCES

Bibliography:
PETRICĂ MARIN, *Ion Luca Caragiale: Bibliografie de recomandare*, 1964, lists the studies published between 1948 and 1962.

General Works:
For Caragiale's life the standard work is ŞERBAN CIOCULESCU, *Viaţa lui I. L. Caragiale* (1940), of which a second edition with three additional chapters appeared in 1969. A shorter work, *I. L. Caragiale*, by the same author appeared in 1967 with the imprint of *Editura*

tineretului. Another biography, fuller than this and easier to read than Cioculescu's *Viaţa* (which is not a connected narrative, but a series of chapters on aspects of the life) is ION ROMAN, *Caragiale* (1964).

Criticism:

CĂLINESCU, G. "Caragiale, omul şi opera" (Caragiale, the Man and His Work), *Studii şi cercetări de istorie literară şi folclor* (Studies and Research in Literary History and Folklore), XI (Bucharest, 1962).

CAZIMIR, ŞTEFAN *Caragiale—universal comic*, (Caragiale—the Comic Universe) (Bucharest, 1967), is an analysis of Caragiale's technique as a comic writer.

CONSTANTINESCU, P. "Cu prilejul reluării 'D-ale carnavalului' " (On the Occasion of the Revival of *D-ale carnavalului*), *Vremea* (Time) (Bucharest, 1935), no. 407.

IBRĂILEANU, G. "Numele proprii în opera comică a lui Caragiale" (Proper Names in the Comic Works of Caragiale) (1926); reprinted in G. Ibrăileanu, *Studii literare* (Literary Studies) (Bucharest, 1957), pp. 123–37. Also "I. L. Caragiale" in G. Ibrăileanu, *Scriitori români şi străini* (Romanian and Foreign Writers) (Jassy, 1926), pp. 38–85, a discussion of *O noapte furtunoasă, Conu Leonida*, and Caragiale's verse.

LOVINESCU, E. In his *Critice*, VI (Bucharest, 1928), 16–35, Lovinescu discusses Caragiale's comedies and *Năpasta*.

MAIORESCU, T. "Comediile lui Caragiale" (Caragiale's Comedies), 1886, reprinted in the collection of Maiorescu's critical essays, *Critice*, III (Bucharest, 1931), 41–54.

VIANU, T. In his *Arta prozatorilor români* (The Art of Romanian Prose Writers) (Bucharest, 1941), pp. 123–39, Vianu analyzes Caragiale's technique in prose.

Index